# Water Skiing on the Amazon

*A Memoir for My Grandchildren*

Patricia S. Taylor Edmisten

JEWELWEED

Copyright © 2014 Patricia S. Taylor Edmisten
All rights reserved.

ISBN: 0692223487
ISBN 13: 9780692223482

*For Sophie and Vincent*

*May you swim with dolphins
and kayak in pristine waters*

**Dolphins**

Pertaining to the family Cetacean,
One of God's stellar creations.
Would I not want to leap so lithely?
Smile so blithely?
Charm with grace and agility?
Outsmart large nets with my mobility?

From *The Treasures of Pensacola Beach,*
by your grandmother

## *Acknowledgements*

**I AM GRATEFUL** for my husband Joe's optimism and unceasing encouragement; for my son, whose life of integrity, compassion, generosity, and diligence has been an inspiration; for my friend Nancy, whose literary insights have guided my writing path over the years; for my neighbor Lydia, who assisted me with the German language; for Tim Smith, valiant computer diagnostician and trouble-shooter, and, especially, for those whose arms that held me.

# Contents

Introduction: The Arms That Held Me .................................................................. xiii
Growing up in the Melting Pot of the Midwest: Milwaukee, Wisconsin ................ 1
Puberty: It's Not Easy ............................................................................................ 11
An All-Woman's High School? You've Got to be Kidding ..................................... 13
Teachers: We Need a Few Good Ones ................................................................. 16
Siblings: Closer Than You Think .......................................................................... 18
Friendship: It Takes Work ..................................................................................... 21
Trust and Gratitude ............................................................................................... 24
Insecurities: Remaining True to Ourselves .......................................................... 25
Hidden Inheritance: On Two of your Great-Grandparents
and Four of your Great-Great Grandparents ....................................................... 27
Things I Wish I Had Not Done ............................................................................. 41
Dating: Attraction, Love, Disappointment, Love ................................................. 43
Choosing a Career Path: The Influence
of Family and Environment .................................................................................. 46
Semper Fi, Always Faithful: Your Grandmother
Joins the Marine Corps ......................................................................................... 48
First Job: So This Is What All That Education Is About ...................................... 49
The Peace Corps: "The Toughest Job You'll Ever Love" ...................................... 50
Peru: The Belly Button of the World .................................................................... 54
Ica, Peru: the Flood ............................................................................................... 64
Peru Mourns: President John F. Kennedy's Assassination .................................. 70
Water Skiing on the Amazon ................................................................................ 71

WATER SKIING ON THE AMAZON

*A Pain in the Butt: The Influence of the
Peace Corps on My Life* ................................................................................... 74

*Graduate Study Followed by Marriage to Papi* ............................................. 76

*Recife, Brazil and the Happiest Day of My Life* ............................................ 78

*Divorce: Finding a New Life with
My Son, Family, and Work* ............................................................................ 82

*Cocoa Beach and the Space Capital of the United States* ........................... 84

*Dr. Patty: The University of Florida* ............................................................. 87

*Dorothy: A Generous and Adventurous Heart* ............................................. 89

*Deep South, Y'all: Mobile and the
University of South Alabama* ........................................................................ 92

*The Cradle of Naval Aviation: Pensacola and the
University of West Florida* ............................................................................ 95

*Nicaragua #1: After the Revolution* ............................................................ 101

*Granddaddy Joe: "The World's Greatest Ecologist"* .................................. 102

*Montezuma's Reward* .................................................................................. 108

*Cuba #1: "The Enemy" Ninety Miles off our Shore* ................................... 111

*Nicaragua #2: Smuggling Censored Newspapers to the Future President* ......... 115

*Religion and Patriotism: a Dangerous Mix* ............................................... 119

*Nicaragua #3: Attending the Inauguration of the First Woman
President in the Americas* ........................................................................... 120

*The United Nations: The Special
Burdens of Poor Women* .............................................................................. 121

*Cuba #2: Befriending "The Enemy" through Student
and Faculty Exchanges* ................................................................................ 123

*Semester at Sea: Circumnavigating the
Earth in One Semester* ................................................................................ *126*

*Cuba #3: Medical Assistance to "The Enemy"* ........................................ *134*

*September 11, 2001: Dissent May Also be Patriotic* ................................ *135*

*In Retrospect: Family, Values, Hard Work, and Faith* ............................ *137*

*Making Difficult Decisions* ........................................................................ *139*

*Treating Ourselves and Others: You Know the Rule* ............................... *140*

*Two Households Can't be Easy, but You're Champions* .......................... *142*

*Faith: The Foundation of My Life* ............................................................ *143*

*In Closing: A Grandmother's Blessing* ..................................................... *147*

## Introduction: The Arms That Held Me

**SOPHIE, THIS YEAR YOU WILL COMPLETE YOUR SIXTEENTH YEAR; VINCENT, YOU WILL COMPLETE YOUR FOURTEENTH, AND I WILL CELEBRATE SEVENTY-FIVE YEARS.** While I'm still in good health, I want to learn, write, travel, and spend lots of time with you and your family. I look forward to many more delicious summers together at our mountain retreat in North Carolina. That said, none of us can take the blessing of life for granted, so I, who have already lived most of my life, want to share with you some family history that, otherwise, may be gone forever. It's all right if, when you start reading this little book, you decide that it's just too much to deal with now, maybe even boring. Should that happen, set it aside, but there will be a time, I promise, when you'll wonder about those who came before you and the ancestral roots that contributed to the people you are today. I can't provide all of the historical tendrils, but others in your family may be able to provide the missing pieces.

My main purpose is not to provide an exhaustive record about your ancestors on my side of the family; it is, instead, to share with you the cultural, spiritual, and ethical environment that helped shape me, and, I think, your father. I've tried to avoid sounding preachy, but I may not always have been successful. You'll find, too, that my narrative isn't always chronological. While I'm writing, something may pop into my head, and I'll insert it where I am at that moment instead of finding the historical place where it might have better fit. I've tried to include the funny and stupid things I've done in my life as well as the stories resulting from decisions of which I'm proud.

I never had the forethought to ask my parents and grandparents the questions for which I now have no answers. It never occurred to me, for example, to ask my grandfathers how it was to leave their birth countries to start a new life in America. The rendering of my parents' and grandparents' stories is not complete because of that shortsightedness. I have folders full of genealogical research and many old family photographs that should be yours one day, but this memoir would have been far more enriching had I thought to ask the questions while they were alive.

# WATER SKIING ON THE AMAZON

As I waded into this memoir, I realized that I had to place some limitations on it or it would go on forever. To what degree, for example, would I include other branches of your immediate family and extended family? If I cast my net too widely, I was sure to offend someone or leave someone out. I would also lose some freedom because I'd have to respect their privacy. As it is, I'm hoping your father will be tolerant of my many references to him and images of him. It would have been impossible, after his birth in 1968, to separate my life from his.

I would have liked to have included more information on Granddaddy Joe's large family and more on his five biological children and their children because they have represented a significant part of my life since we married in 1984. Here again, I've had to limit the scope of my writing and remind myself that this work is my memoir and not a comprehensive genealogical record. It starts with my ancestral roots and the life that emerged from those roots.

One more point before I begin: After innumerable readings of this memoir, I realize that some of the content may read like political essays, especially the sections that deal with Nicaragua, Cuba, and Semester at Sea. That material, however, also reflects my values and world experiences and tells you about the grandmother you have right now, not the child, girl, or student she used to be. I've certainly not "talked" down to you. I hope that, years from now, you'll be grateful that I didn't. I give you permission to skip what seems too heavy now. You may wish to let the Table of Contents guide you. If you decide to skip the sections I mentioned, be sure that you pick up the last five.

# PATRICIA S. TAYLOR EDMISTEN

WITH MY FATHER, JOHN EUGENE SILKE, AGE TWENTY-THREE, 1939

WATER SKIING ON THE AMAZON

WITH MY PARENTS, DOROTHY ELEANORE SILKE AND JOHN EUGENE SILKE, 1939

## *Growing up in the Melting Pot of the Midwest: Milwaukee, Wisconsin*

**I HAVE FOND MEMORIES OF MY OLD NEIGHBORHOOD.** We lived in an attractive apartment above our grandparents' bakery and pastry shop at 4233 W. North Avenue. Back then it was common for people to live above family-owned shops. Our neighborhood always seemed alive, and you didn't have to get in your car, like we do today, to buy a loaf of bread or some meat for supper. Our block was lined with a pharmacy, butcher shop, beauty parlor, doctor's office, and Grandpa Henry's pastry shop. On the next block was the "beer depot," where my brother and I would return our empty bottles, mostly soda, because no one knew how unhealthy it was. People wouldn't think of throwing away a bottle then. Beer and soda companies sterilized them and re-used them. This was well before beverages came in cans. You returned the empty bottles to get back the deposit you had earlier paid in case you never troubled to return them. Sometimes we'd get to keep the deposit for the movies or candy.

Your great-great grandfather, Henry Seitz, foreground, in his first shop, Milwaukee, 1910, approx.

THE SECOND SEITZ BAKERY, NEWLY REMODELED, MY MOTHER, THIRD FROM RIGHT, HER SISTER CATHERINE, FIRST ON LEFT, 1935

In 1937, after saving for many years, my grandparents built a beautiful home in what was then a rural area known by the Indian name, Wauwatosa. (It is now a large, vibrant suburb of Milwaukee, and their beautiful home still shines on lovely tree-lined Swan Boulevard). After moving, my grandparents continued to work in the bakery, beginning their day at 4:00 a.m., and ending after 6:00 in the evening.

Many of the customers who visited the bakery spoke languages other than English because they or their parents had emigrated from Germany, Poland, Italy, Scandinavia, and even a family from the Netherlands, the home of your lovely step-mom. Although my grandmother, who was born in Milwaukee, understood and spoke German, it was Grandpa's first language, and he never lost his accent.

I'll interject here with a little story: When I was four, I became very sick with a high fever, and I developed a huge lump on the side of my neck. It was scarlet fever, a potentially lethal infection back then. When the disease was finally diagnosed, I was placed in a little glass isolation room inside of the children's ward in the hospital. I remember receiving the gift of a Scarlet O'Hara doll from my grandparents. You may know that Scarlet O'Hara is the name of the female protagonist of Margaret Mitchell's famous novel, *Gone with the Wind*, set in Georgia during the Civil War. (Do watch the movie if you haven't seen it.) When I left the hospital on a beautiful spring day, I was told that I ran into my grandfather's arms and said in German, *"Wie grün alles ist!"* (How green everything is.) So I must have been listening to my grandparents speaking German to one another and probably spoke a little myself. I wanted my doll but the nurse explained that they had to burn everything that I had touched.

Grandpa was a superb baker who specialized in rich pastries, always made with butter, of course, as well as cakes and hearty breads. He was famous for his wedding cakes, and, despite having enormous, muscular hands from all the dough he kneaded, he would decorate his cakes with exquisite roses, leaves, and vines. I didn't realize how special it was to have my grandfather bake my birthday cake every year, but I loved it, when as a little girl, he'd lift me up to his cake decorating table and let me watch him work. Sometimes he'd squeeze a little frosting on my fingers for me to lick.

Every morning but Sunday my mother would send my brother or me down to the bakery for fresh hard rolls for our breakfast that tasted like warm French bread. We loved to eat them with butter and jam. Another treat were the *schnecks*, long, yeasty sweet rolls with *streusel* and dribbles of butter frosting on the top. Years later, when I was in high school and working part-time in the bakery, I waited on a small, chubby woman who wore a *babushka*, a scarf, around her head. She asked me in heavily accented English, "*how much for schnecks?*" I told her, "Two for .25 cents." She replied, "W*ell den, gib me.*" (Now one *schneck* would probably cost at least $2.50. at Starbucks.)

Although not wealthy, our neighborhood was safe and clean. When our friends invited us to play, they would shout outside our house and yell, "Oh Patty, Oh Johnny" for my brother and me to come out. We played "Kick the

Can" in the alleys or "Pom Pom Pull Away Let Your Horses Run Away" in the corner park next to our building or in an empty field at the "car barns," where the public busses were kept overnight. For the most part, our parents didn't worry about our safety. They knew other parents wouldn't hesitate to intervene if some child were misbehaving. There were a few rules, however: We'd have to be in our houses when the street lights came on, for example, and we could not talk back unless we wanted a good spanking.

During the summer, we could play after supper and still have plenty of daylight before the street lights came on. Our play time was short during the winter months, although, if our homework was done, we could go ice skating at nearby Washington Park, if some of the older kids were with us. We skated to Strauss waltzes piped out over the frozen lagoon with ice that shone a silvery blue. We also played "Crack the Whip," where a long line of skaters would hold hands, going as fast as they could, one behind the other. After reaching the fastest possible speed, the leader, usually a strong young man, would execute a quick turn, leaving the rest of the skaters to fan out on a wild ride, with the last few flying over the ice.

Because our apartment was small by today's standards (two adults and two children in a two-bedroom, one-bath dwelling), my parents arranged to celebrate our birthdays at Milwaukee parks. Mom would make her famous pot-roasted chicken and German potato salad, and Grandpa would bake a special cake. Relatives would drive, and our friends would pile in their cars. There would always be a playground, but sometimes there would only be a clean stream with stepping stones that invited us to imagine ourselves as explorers.

I never questioned our social/economic standing in the community because no one in our neighborhood had a lot of money. All the mothers stayed home to be with the small children or to tend to household duties, and, if there were a family car, there would be only one. None of my friends' families took vacations away from home. Ours was the first when we rented a cabin on Lake Nokomis in northern Wisconsin for a week or two during the summer, a practice we maintained until we started traveling to Florida.(I dreaded using the outhouse in the dead of night.)

One night at the cabin, we were all hiding from a bat that was frantically circling in the kitchen. My grandmother, your great- great-grandmother Kuni, the only brave one among us, my father and grandfather having stayed in the city to work, covered her hair with one hand, and with the other, went after that bat with a rolled up newspaper. She covered her hair because she believed that if the bat got into it, she'd never get it out of the tangle. It was on Lake Nokomis that Dad taught Uncle John and me to fish with cane poles and worms. I caught a giant Northern with that pole, or so its size seemed to me. Many years later, I introduced your father to fishing from bridges over the Indian and Banana Rivers when we lived in Cocoa Beach, Florida.

When I was eleven, my parents started taking us out of school just before Easter vacation, and we would drive from still wintry Milwaukee to tropical Miami Beach. We were the envy of our friends who had never left Wisconsin. The first time I watched the "mermaids" at Weeki Wachee Springs I decided that, one day, I would be a mermaid and live in Florida.

Uncle John and I vividly recall Dad waking us at dawn on the morning of our departure with the question, "Any one for Florida?" His happiness and energy before these trips was contagious. Mom would have prepared surprise boxes for us that held coloring books, crayons, comic books, and snacks so we could entertain ourselves during the 1,600- mile car trip. Like young children everywhere, my parents frequently heard their share of "How much longer?" or "When are we going to be there?"

It's not a stretch to say that my family's yearly trips to Florida probably influenced the circumstances under which your parents met, and subsequently, the place where your father and step-mom met. In fact, my grandparents started visiting Florida in the mid 1930s, once their bakery business was thriving. Their Florida road trips, in turn, influenced my mother's love of your native state. So, if you ever wonder how you and your brother came to be born in Florida instead of Wisconsin, for example, just think of your great-great-grandparents, Kuni and Henry, and of your great-grandparents, Dorothy and John. This is just one example of how pieces of family history influence our lives in ways that remain invisible unless we ask the questions.

# WATER SKIING ON THE AMAZON

Returning to Milwaukee, our lives were circumscribed by family, St. Anne's Catholic Church, and our neighborhood. There were always gatherings with grandparents, aunts, uncles, and cousins to celebrate birthdays and the holidays. We attended St. Anne's School, a mile from our house. Every class was taught by a sister, most of whom were good teachers and caring women, although occasionally there was a mean one we'd dread getting.

When I was in first grade, and didn't know the difference between a kind sister and a mean or misguided one, something possessed me to make a low humming sound from my desk in the first row of seats. Nothing was visible on my lips, and the sister didn't know who was making the strange noise. She yanked up the little boy next to me, thinking it was he who made the offensive sound and stood him under a picture of a crying baby. When I think of when my tendency to challenge unjust authority began, I think it was then. I raised my hand and told the sister that the boy hadn't made the noise, that I was the guilty one. Instead of rewarding my honesty, she stood me under the picture of the crying baby, my first public humiliation.

Dad drove us to school in the mornings on his way to work, but, unless the weather was awful, we'd walk back home for lunch and then walk back to school for the afternoon session. Finally, we walked home after the school day. On snowy or rainy days, we carried lunch boxes but still walked home at the end of the school day, sometimes balancing on the top of snow banks, hungry and cold. (I still remember the smell of those tin lunch boxes, a smell that never went away, even after scrubbing.)

My brother and I shared a double bed in the small front bedroom till I was about ten. My parents shared the second bedroom that was only a little bigger than ours. One day I came home from school and found that there were two "Hollywood" beds along the wall of the dining room. Hollywood beds were basically twin beds made to look like sofas because of the decorative covers and pillows used to disguise them. We got used to the beds in the dining room that had previously been used for special dinners and a place to do homework. My parents had given up their bedroom so we'd each have our own, a sacrifice that was lost on us.

I don't remember getting an allowance, but I do remember my chores. Each week I'd scrub the many stairs leading up to our apartment from the street entrance. "On my knees" seems exaggerated now, but that's how I did it, with a bucket of hot, soapy water and a strong rag, the way my mother showed me. She also taught me how to iron my father's shirts, how to sprinkle them with water before ironing, and which part of the shirt to iron first, next, etc. Then there was the daily dish washing and drying and weekly dusting and laundry. Because we had no back yard, only a place for trucks to make deliveries to the bakery, we had to hang our clothes in the basement to dry. Mom would carry the laundry down the staircase to the street below, pass in front of the bakery, turn the corner, walk down the "gangway" to the side entrance, and descend the stairs to the basement. Each apartment had a separate storage room down there, and it was a dark and scary place to a child. I still think of how easy I have it now with a washer and dryer in a separate laundry room inside my house. Still, on sunny days, I hang our clothes outside on the line. In fact, that's one chore I've come to love, especially in our mountain home when I lift up my eyes to the green mountain behind our house and sometimes see a hawk circling above.

In thinking about the division of labor between my brother and me, I was having trouble remembering a single chore my brother had, so I called him. He laughed, thinking at first that he was given none. Gradually, however, Uncle John recalled some chores, reassuring me that, when he was old enough, he took turns doing the dishes. As he got older, he helped carry laundry for our mother. In the winter, he helped my father put up storm windows on all the upstairs windows, a dangerous job because of the tall ladder Dad had to climb, while sliding the window upward, mindful always of the concrete sidewalk below. My brother also washed the car when he was older. So, he's redeemed. I thought there might have been some gender discrimination going on.

After my grandparents moved to their new home, Grandpa surprised Grandma with an ebony Baby Grand piano. Grandma was one of eleven children in a family that loved music. Back then it was common for families to gather in the living room after supper to enjoy an evening of music. Grandma played beautifully but had to give up her music during those initial hard years in the bakery. When I was nine or so, she bought a piano for me and paid for a teacher to come to our apartment once a week.

The lady was pleasant and probably a good teacher, but I hated to practice. Grandma threatened to sell the piano if I didn't practice. The piano was gone when I came home from school one afternoon. Now I wish I had been more disciplined.

Miss Muffet was our first pet. She was entirely white, with a pink nose and blue eyes. We didn't have her long because she escaped down the long stairs and out the door into the street where she was run over. We were forlorn without her, but soon Snooper, another female, joined the family. We named our first dog *Snooper* because she behaved like a hunting dog with her nose always to the ground. Adopted from the humane society, Snooper looked like a mix of German Shepherd and innumerable other breeds. She was uncontrollable. We took her to dog obedience school, hoping we could make her behave like other dogs we knew, dogs who would allow you to pet them without jumping all over you, dogs who wouldn't tear through the formal lily garden in the center of the park next door, uprooting plants and scattering soil, dogs who would come when called.

At dog obedience school, Snooper refused to come out from under the bench when she saw all those other dogs lined up on the floor, dogs that were more refined than she. When we tried to pull her out from her hiding place under a bench, Snooper straightened her front legs and resisted. We yanked on her leash till she slid out, her legs stiff, unyielding. We left dog obedience school with our heads almost as low as Snooper's.

AGE TEN, WITH OUR PUPPY SNOOPER, MILWAUKEE, 1949

One afternoon we came home from school to find that Snooper was not there to greet us. Mom explained that a "farmer" wanted her, and that she'd be much happier on a farm than in our apartment. We cried and whined for days, till our parents relented and took us to the humane society to reclaim her. (I don't remember how Mom explained that lie.) Snooper was so excited to see us. She may not have been trained in social niceties, but she was house trained. That poor, sweet dog had not peed during the three days she was in the shelter. When we got her outside, she had the longest pee in history. It wasn't long after that, however, that we came home from school and found that Snooper was gone for good. Now Mom was a tower of strength against all our wheedling and begging.

As compensation for having lost our dog, we adopted another female cat. We named her Pincus after "Uncle Pincus," the TV character from the popular Mollie Goldberg TV show. Our new cat was a Calico, a collage of black, white, and brown, each color distinct, no colors running together, as if an artist had experimented with bold colors on a canvas of cat. Even as a mature cat, Pincus loved to suck on a pink flannel blanket, while she kneaded it with her paws, as if she were still a nursing kitten. While she sucked, she PURRED.

## *Puberty: It's Not Easy*

**BY SEVENTH GRADE, DESPITE THE VIGILANCE OF THE NUNS, BOYS AND GIRLS IN MY SCHOOL STARTED NOTICING EACH OTHER.** It was a time of insecurity, when we were discovering our own identities. During those early teen years, much of how we see ourselves is influenced by those around us, especially our friends. It's not till later, if we're thoughtful persons, that we begin to define ourselves through our own values and experiences. That dependence on what others think of us can be paralyzing if we're unaware of what's going on.

In eighth grade, as we edged closer to high school, my friends and I explored this new and emerging attraction to the opposite sex by having "spin the bottle" parties. I don't know how we got away with this game, but our trusting parents never checked on our basement gatherings in which one person—the person last kissed—would spin a milk bottle and kiss the boy or girl it pointed to, or vice versa. We'd go into a separate room and tentatively kiss each other, lips closed of course, pretending to hold the kiss long enough to impress the other kids. I can't believe that I kissed some guy I probably didn't even like. I sure would have been upset if I had known that your father had been doing the same thing when he was my age. Sr. Mary Ladislaus (named after a Polish saint) found out about our parties and warned us about behaving impurely. We never did learn who the spy among us was.

I think you've heard the next story before, but it comes from the same time period. Although we were the first in our neighborhood to own a TV (with a small, greenish screen), we still attended weekend movies, a popular form of family entertainment. My parents went regularly when they were dating, and, when we were children, they would give Uncle John and me a quarter each to see a double feature, most of them cowboy and Tarzan movies. When I was in eighth grade, Tom put his arm around me in the theater. Unknown to us, my brother was crouching in the seat behind. You can just imagine his glee and facial expression when he announced his presence with "I'm going to tell Mom and Dad on you unless you give me some money." So Tom paid off your Uncle John to get rid of him. This is the kind of thing I had to put up with throughout my grade school years. He stopped being a pest when he entered high school, but then there were other concerns, and he can tell you what I mean. Still, after all my complaints about my brother, all the nasty tricks he played on me, all the trouble he got into, my love and appreciation for him continues to grow.

Another amusing anecdote, that was not funny at the time, happened after my mother sat me down at our kitchen table to tell me "the facts of life." Apparently, I wasn't ready because I fled from the table after she told me. Even though I had thought my friend Barbara more sophisticated than I, when I revealed to her what Mom had told me about how babies were conceived, she grimaced and said, "I don't believe it!" It sounds improbable, but this event must have occurred when we were already in seventh grade. (Children learn about the "birds and the bees" much earlier now, given all the explicit TV and movies that are available to them.)

YOUR GREAT-UNCLE, JOHN MICHAEL SILKE, AGE FIFTEEN, 1957

## *An All-Woman's High School? You've Got to be Kidding*

**I ATTENDED A NEW CATHOLIC HIGH SCHOOL IN WHAT WAS THEN CONSIDERED "THE COUNTRY," WEST OF MILWAUKEE.** Barbara, who lived near me, boarded the bus at the stop after mine. For four years we shared the same seat on that bus. I wonder what we talked about all that time.

Most of the new girls I met came from different backgrounds than those with whom I attended grade school. A Catholic education was highly valued, not only for the quality of instruction, but also because parents wanted their children to have religious education in their ancestral faith. But many of the families from my neighborhood couldn't afford private school tuition. Here's where my mothers' parents helped out again. They not only paid for my high school tuition but also for most of my college tuition at Catholic Marquette University.

There are certain advantages to attending a single sex school: My friends and I didn't have to worry about impressing boys at Divine Savior. I could raise my hand in class without fear that I would embarrass myself in front of them. Also, we didn't have to worry if we were dressed stylishly because we wore uniforms, not the kind students wear today, where you have some choice as to the color of shirts you wear. We wore Navy blue gabardine skirts, white blouses with Peter Pan (round) collars, and a bolero, a sort of loose vest without buttons. I have to conclude that the only reason we had to wear those boleros was to cover our breasts.

WITH BARBARA, FRESHMAN YEAR, AGE FOURTEEN, 1953

Feminine modesty was considered a virtue in my school. Toward that end, Mom and I searched for the perfect gown for my junior prom. Mine was a gorgeous, expensive thing, with layers of white tulle, the kind of material used in bridal veils. The gown was strapless, so Mom bought additional white tulle and tacked one end of it to the gown above one breast, brought it over my shoulders, and tacked it to the other side. When we got to the beautifully decorated school gym, the nuns separated us from our dates and inspected each one of us to see that we were modestly dressed. The sisters were prepared with scarves or other cover-ups to put over our shoulders if we failed the test. They also recommended that we visit the Virgin Mary's shrine with our dates to pray for purity after the prom (no necking).

For me, not knowing whom to invite to the prom was the worst part. Would it have been any better at a co-ed high school? How awful to have to wait by the phone, hoping some guy—any guy—would invite you. My mom suggested that I invite Donnie, a boy who lived in our neighborhood, a nice boy, a good boy, and a very dull boy. But I couldn't miss the junior prom, and so I got up the nerve, picked up the phone, and invited him. I think proms are over-rated.

With my date, junior prom, age seventeen (Pet "Pincus" on chair), 1956

## *Teachers: We Need a Few Good Ones*

**MY HIGH SCHOOL HAD ONLY FOUR HUNDRED OR SO STUDENTS, UNLIKE YOURS, THAT, AT THIS WRITING, HAS 1,724 STUDENTS (WIKIPEDIA), SO IT WAS EASIER FOR ME TO FIND A SPECIAL TEACHER WHOM I TRUSTED.** My favorite teacher was Miss Wargin. (We didn't use "Ms.") Miss Wargin was a tall, thin, elegant woman who taught Spanish, and she was one of the few teachers in our school who was not a Catholic sister. Reminiscing, I've seen more clearly how certain individuals in our past can influence our futures. Would I have chosen to study Spanish in college without having known Miss Wargin? Probably not, because I already had the required two years of a foreign language (Latin) and two years of Spanish by the time I entered Marquette. But Miss Wargin had inspired me to learn about countries where Spanish was spoken. Five years after taking my last course with her, I was able to place into an advanced Spanish language class during Peace Corps training at Cornell University. I also remember that Miss Wargin came to visit me when I was hospitalized, at age fifteen, with an undiagnosed blood disorder. She helped me to believe in myself at a time when I was emotionally insecure.

How does a student make a connection with such a teacher? I can't speak for others, but when I was teaching at the university level, I came to appreciate it when students made the effort to meet with me. Sometimes they were experiencing personal problems that prevented them from completing an assignment. Some of them had conflicts at home, had been ill, or were raising children. Some would ask if they could re-take an exam or have an extension on a paper that was due. I always tried to accommodate those students in some way, assuming they were being honest and not trying to take advantage. Sometimes, in fairness to the other students, I'd reduce their grade somewhat. There were other students, however, who fell behind but never kept me informed. They gave the impression that their grades didn't matter, even though they might have cared a lot. So, if you have problems keeping up with your assignments, try to communicate early with your teachers and see if a compromise can be arranged. The students that I came to know personally became more real to me. They had names and lives apart from school, and I knew that they were taking their classes seriously.

John Steinbeck, a famous American writer (*The Grapes of Wrath*, *Cannery Row*), spoke about the importance of finding *real* teachers:

> It is customary for adults to forget how hard and dull and long school is. The learning by memory all the basic things one must know is the most incredible and unending effort. Learning to read is probably the most difficult and revolutionary thing that happens to the human brain and if you don't believe that, watch an illiterate adult try to do it. School is not easy and it is not for the most part very much fun, but then, if you are very lucky, you may find a teacher. Three real teachers in a lifetime is the best of luck. I have come to believe that a great teacher is a great artist and that there are as few as there are any other great artists. Teaching might even be the greatest of the arts since the medium is the human mind and spirit. My three had these things in common—they all loved what they were doing. They did not tell—they catalyzed a burning desire to know. Under their influence, the horizons sprung wide and fear went away and the unknown became knowable. But most important of all, the truth, that dangerous stuff, became beautiful and very precious."

Sophie and Vincent, I hope you will each find at least three teachers like the kind John Steinbeck described.

## *Siblings:* Closer Than You Think

**IT OCCURRED TO ME THAT YOUR RELATIONSHIP WITH EACH OTHER IS NOT UNLIKE MY EARLY RELATIONSHIP WITH MY BROTHER, YOUR UNCLE JOHN.** You are nearly two years apart, and my brother and I are three years apart. As older sisters, you and I, Sophie, have had to put up with a lot of our brothers' mischief. Of course we love them, and if they needed us, we'd be there for them, although I recall a time I would not have said anything so generous.

When I was a new teen, and we still lived in the apartment above the bakery, I heard a noise outside the bathroom door while I was taking a bath. I cried out, and my parents caught my brother spying at me through the keyhole. I was mortified and angry. We all need to set boundaries for ourselves. Some boundaries are physical; some emotional. It's easier to get along with one another when we respect those boundaries.

My brother means the world to me now. In addition to our shared familial backgrounds, we are also closer genetically to each other than to anyone else in the world, like the two of you. And you've got to admit, Sophie, that, despite the times you may feel like throwing something at him, Vincent is a *mensch*, a bright, decent, basically generous, frequently funny brother who I'm convinced loves you very much.

YOUR GREAT-GRANDFATHER JOHN, 44; GRANDMOTHER, 20; GREAT-UNCLE, JOHN, 17, CHRISTMAS, 1959

Left to right, Jana, Aunt Lana, your dad, 18 years,
Uncle John, me, Granddaddy Joe, and Pam, 1986

With Uncle John, Granddaddy, Aunt Lana, "Fox & Hounds," Wisconsin, 2013.

Vincent, sometimes it must seem that you and your sister are always squabbling over something. Her interests are bound to be different from yours, so you'll rarely agree on what you'd like to do together as a family. You might want to fish, for example; she might prefer to stay home and read. Or she wants to visit Universal Studios and the new Harry Potter exhibit, and you want to stay at home and work on your aquarium. During times like these your parents try to help you reach a compromise, a solution where everyone gives up a little to have something else you can all agree upon.

Sophie may not tell you, Vincent, as siblings your ages rarely do, that she loves you, but she does. I remember taking you to see the pediatrician when your parents were working, and you and Sophie didn't have school. Sophie and I were waiting for the results of your chest X-ray. When we learned that you had pneumonia, she was visibly worried and asked me if you'd pull through. I've also seen her take time, without complaint, from her own homework to help you with yours. And I've seen you help her with her fishing tackle when she has problems. These are just a few of the ways brothers and sisters support each other and show their love.

## *Friendship: It Takes Work*

**I MENTIONED EARLIER THAT BARBARA WAS MY BEST FRIEND, AND SHE LIVED ONLY TWO BLOCKS FROM ME.** Because Barbara had three older sisters, she always seemed to be more "cool" than I. Sometimes I'd spend the night at Barbara's house, and we'd sit around the kitchen table while her older sisters were getting ready to go out dancing. We'd watch them apply their make-up and hear about the guys they liked, all of whom were excellent dancers. We couldn't wait to join them when they went to the Roof and Eagles Ballrooms. Because we were too young, Barbara and I practiced our dancing at her house. And at school, after lunch, the nuns would let us dance in a hall, next to the cafeteria. We played vinyl records on the phonograph and practiced the jitterbug and cha-cha. Barbara and I eventually became pretty accomplished dancers.

We were not always in the same classes, but we ate our lunch together every day. Other friends would join us. Kathy was a girl I knew since first grade, and while we weren't friends then, we became close in high school, and we're still close. She has become an admired and respected visual artist. Ann also joined our lunch table. She was the daughter of a physician of Polish descent and lived in a mansion on Lake Drive in Milwaukee. She had ten siblings. Ann's house was so big that her parents allowed her to have several friends over at a time for "pajama parties." We stayed up till all hours, dancing, eating, and talking. Years later, I tried to keep up the friendship with Ann, but she pretty much went her own way. Sometimes I have the tendency to reach out to old friends more than they do to me. But when I finally get the message that they're not interested in maintaining the friendship, I take the hint and let them go, trying not to take it personally, although it's hard not to be disappointed.

Barbara was still in high school when her father died. I remember how one night she stood at our apartment door, so forlorn. We embraced her, and she spent the evening with my family. Later, my parents invited Barbara to accompany us on two of our road trips to Miami Beach, and, during our senior year, she accompanied us on a trip to Las Vegas and California.

(Barbara's sisters loaned us their identification cards so that we could get into the floor shows at the night clubs.) Please don't try that.

Now when I visit Uncle John and Aunt Lana in Wisconsin, I try to keep those old friendships alive by visiting Barbara, Kathy, and Connie. Connie and I met on the Sherman bus on the first day of classes at Marquette University. We were both insecure and didn't know how to navigate the campus. Those first tentative minutes of interaction on a public bus grew into an enduring friendship.

Since moving to Pensacola with your father, when he was nine-years-old, I've made a few friends "of the heart." I've learned that the friendships worth keeping require a lot of attention, like a garden. If there are things that get in the way, like misunderstandings or arguments (the weeds), we need to make things right. If there have been long spells without contact, we have to reach out, even if we fear we might be rejected (water). If a friend needs our support, we must be ready with comforting words and hugs (the sun).

I've learned that most of us have this in common: We want to feel that our lives matter to others, that we have something to contribute, and that we are basically good people. (Over the years, I've also observed that if you're a good listener, people will think you're an amazing conversationalist, even though you might say little.)

There was a girl in high school with whom I didn't communicate unless it was to give her a perfunctory greeting. "Brenda's" uniform was frequently dirty, her hair tangled, and she smelled a little. She also seemed to have some kind of speech impediment. Even though we didn't know anything about her circumstances, my friends and I tended to avoid her. As I look back, I wish I had befriended her. Although I felt sorry for her and was never mean to her, I was comfortable with my own little group, and while we thought we were all kind young women, I don't think a single one of us ever reached out to her. Since then, when I meet people who are different from me and/or my culture, even though it might involve taking a risk, I try to strike up a conversation with them, and usually I'm the one who profits from the encounter.

I realize how communication avenues have changed since I was your age, when we might have talked for hours on the phone. Although I realize the benefits texting offers, we do lose much of the human quality of conversation. I can't see your face if you're sad, for example. I can't hear your voice that might tell me how you're feeling. I can't see how you'll respond to the words "I'm sorry" to see if you're relieved or angry. I don't know if you're afraid. Texting condenses who we are to a few brief words, and our momentary happiness is reduced to a to a smiley face. Is there a symbol that represents sadness? I don't know. Texting can appear curt, unfeeling, and, like with e-mail, there's a lot of opportunity for misunderstanding. Yet I admit to being grateful for the opportunity to send you both an occasional text, telling you I'm thinking about you, or congratulating you on your good grades. Then this summer, after we took you to the airport in Charlotte, you used texting to assure us that you had found the right gate, and, a few minutes later, that you had boarded the plane. I then texted you that we would remain in the airport till you had departed. We were relieved, two hours later, with the text we received saying you had safely arrived. How great is that!

## *Trust and Gratitude*

**YOU'D THINK, AT MY AGE, THAT MY PERSONALITY WOULD ALREADY HAVE BEEN FULLY FORMED, THAT I AM NOW THE PERSON I HAVE WANTED TO BECOME, BUT IT ISN'T SO.** There are qualities I wish I had cultivated when I was your age, like, for example, trust and gratitude. I'm still learning to trust that any problems I might have will be solved in time. I'm still learning to trust God and myself. It's also easy to distrust our family members, friends, and teachers. We may think they're not treating us fairly or that they expect too much of us. When you find yourself slipping into this negative way of thinking, or "stinking thinking," it's good to put a positive slant on the issue and give the other party the benefit of the doubt.

Even now I need to trust that I'm being a good wife, mother, step-mother, mother-in-law, grandmother, and friend. Also, I wish I had more frequently expressed appreciation to others for the small and large gifts in my life. Expressions of gratitude tell others that their efforts have not been lost on us, that they had meaning, that they uplifted us, and affected our lives in a positive way. And, if a gift we received wasn't appropriate, expressions of gratitude still let the giver know we appreciated that they were thinking of us. In a way, thanking people keeps us a bit humble because it forces us to see that all the benefits we enjoy are not of our own making. And prayer is a way to thank God for the loved ones who physically and emotionally sustain us every day, "the arms that hold us."

## *Insecurities: Remaining True to Ourselves*

**PERHAPS BECAUSE OF MY HEIGHT, MY POSTURE, OR THE WAY I SPOKE, OTHER STUDENTS OFTEN THOUGHT THAT I WAS MORE CONFIDENT THAN I WAS.** I was pretty good at sports and played varsity basketball and volleyball, and I was a decent student, making As, Bs, and an occasional C, but I doubted myself. Where that self-doubt came from, I don't know. Perhaps it began when, as a girl of nine or ten, I put on weight due to all those goodies from Grandpa's bakery, and, as a result, some nasty boys in my neighborhood teased or taunted by saying, "Fatty Patty" as I walked by. That early humiliation and embarrassment stayed with me long after I had grown taller and slimmer. I think all young people have some issue with their bodies, mostly imagined, made worse by advertising that promotes the perfect build, flawless skin, and perfect hair. We're told not to worry about those images, not to let them affect our self-esteem, but it's harder when you're young and want to be accepted. Thankfully, by age thirteen, I started to grow taller and slimmer.

In high school, there were students who always seemed confident. You could see they were used to having what they wanted. They hung out together, talked louder, laughed more, and were more aggressive in sports. They exuded an aura of superiority, even if they didn't intend it. (Maybe I'm imagining it, but these students also seemed to come from the wealthiest families.)

There's still a disparity between how others perceive me and how I perceive myself, although now I'm less likely to care. That said, I'm still uncomfortable in certain social settings. I don't like small talk, the kind you need to survive at cocktail parties. If I know the people and have something in common—politics—for example, I'm fine. Thankfully, I've learned a few helpful tricks. If I feel out-of-place, I act as if I belong and remind myself to act confidently. Most of the time, I forget that I've been acting, and I relax, ultimately enjoying myself.

Speaking of pretending, I'm reminded of the time my mother's girl scout troop went to a live variety show on WTMJ - TV, a local Milwaukee channel. Girl scouts, brownies, boy scouts, and cub scouts had been invited. Toward the end of the show, the host (cruelly, I later decided) asked the two tallest girl scouts to come up to the stage and for the two shortest cub scouts to do likewise. My mother urged me to go forward, but I was apprehensive. When I got on the stage, the host paired me with a short cub scout, and he explained to the audience that both "couples" would dance the jitterbug. The audience, through their applause, would decide which pair won. I could not have been more than eleven and was still chubby. Also, I was clueless about dancing, but I had watched young people jitterbug on TV, and so I took control, leading the younger scout in one made-up move after another. Finally, wearing my green girl scout uniform with its badges, I picked him up under his arms and twirled him around. The audience roared their approval, and we won. I received a gift certificate for a dress at an upscale store. I trusted my impulse and took a risk, despite my fears.

 I recall another time when I pretended: Betty, a girl who lived in our neighborhood, had a birthday party to which all the other children had been invited. I was crushed that she had not invited me. I wanted to go, and I went. Rifling through my books to find the most presentable one, I appeared at the birthday girl's door with the gently used book in a brown paper bag. Her mother came to the door, smiled, and invited me to join the other children who were playing a game that required one to drop clothes pins into a milk bottle. In retrospect, it's as if a stranger, not I, had been the interloper.

# Hidden Inheritance:
## On Two of your Great-Grandparents and Four of your Great-Great Grandparents

**I STILL MISS MY PARENTS, AND I STILL OCCASIONALLY CRY WHEN I THINK OF HOW GOOD THEY WERE TO UNCLE JOHN AND ME.** How I wish you had known them, and how they would have loved you. When I was in high school, my mom, your great grandmother, would frequently surprise me with new clothes she thought I'd love. I'd get home from school, and she would have displayed them on my bed as a surprise. She did this despite the fact that our family never had a lot of money. Dad would get upset with Mom when she'd show him the bills on Tuesdays, when he got paid. Mom never kept good records of what bills had and had not been paid, so this issue was a source of tension throughout their marriage. Maybe that's why I've been so careful about not accruing too much debt and paying my bills on time.

Dorothy was a stylish, fun-loving young woman who fell deeply in love with your great-grandfather John when she was eighteen. He was still seventeen and on the Varsity football team. Sometime I'd love to go over the old photo albums with you because they made such an elegant couple, looking as if they had just stepped out of the movies that were made during the 1930s and 1940s. Dorothy was tall and slim, with flashing dark eyes. John was over six feet, handsome, athletic, and romantic.

MY MOTHER (YOUR GREAT-GRANDMOTHER), DOROTHY ELEANORE SEITZ, 18 YEARS, 1933

# WATER SKIING ON THE AMAZON

In 1938, when she was twenty-three, just before marrying my father, Mom traveled from Milwaukee to Miami by Greyhound bus with her first cousin, Celia. After a few days in Miami, they crossed the Florida Straits on an amphibian plane and visited Cuba for a week. I had always wondered why these cousins chose to visit Cuba at such a young age until I found a package of postcards written in the early 1930s by my grandmother Kuni, your great-great grandmother, who wrote the cards during a road trip she and my grandfather Henry had taken to Florida. Among them was a postcard from Havana. So, even within their modest financial circumstances, first my grandparents, and later, my mother, found a way to explore the island-nation of Cuba. (Your dad now has those historic postcards from Miami and Havana.)

MY FATHER (YOUR GREAT-GRANDFATHER), JOHN EUGENE SILKE, 1933

My mother's trip to Cuba led to her love of Latin music and an appreciation of Spanish-speaking people that made it easier for her to later support my decision to go to Peru with the Peace Corps. With my three visits to Cuba at this writing, the tradition continues.

Mom, like most mothers back then, stayed at home during the day, although sometimes, to earn a little extra income, she helped in the bakery downstairs. She always had dinner waiting when Dad came home from work. She was an excellent cook, although meals tended to be on the heavy side with meat, potatoes, gravy, one vegetable, salad, and dessert.

In 1956, when I was sixteen, and Uncle John was thirteen, Mom talked Dad into driving from Milwaukee to Mexico City and then on to Acapulco on the Pacific coast. The arduous trip to Mexico City took a week. You'd have to consult a map to appreciate the distance. We didn't stay long in Mexico City because I was stricken with altitude sickness. In Acapulco, we stayed at the Del Monte, a gorgeous hotel with tropical gardens, on top of a cliff overlooking the Pacific. I was in heaven, especially when a U.S. Navy ship came into port carrying handsome young sailors, wearing jaunty white uniforms, who made their way to the bar and pool at our hotel.

After the grueling trip home, Dad was so relieved he said that Okinawa (World War II) and Mexico were enough foreign travel for a life-time, and that he'd never leave the U.S. again. He didn't, and neither did my mom, although I'm sure she would have loved to have continued her international adventures. Now consider that, at your young ages, you've already been to Europe three times and to Costa Rica once.

Dad reported for duty one morning while it was still dark. I remember that Mom and I watched him waiting for his bus at the street corner, standing in a pool of light from the street lamp. Mom was crying hard. I put my arm around her and cried too. He was the perfect father, much like your own dad. He was a hard worker who loved and trusted us to be good children.

You may recall the photo I gave your father of great-grandpa John seated on top of a large earth-moving machine in Okinawa, the Japanese island in the Pacific where a major World War II battle was fought. Dad wasn't drafted until most of the fighting was over because he had two children. Although he didn't see combat, as part of the "clean-up" crew, he certainly witnessed its horrors. Like many returning veterans, however, he never spoke of them. (Uncle John has the album containing your great-grandfather's letters and photos from that time period.)

Dad was a man of deep faith who never missed Mass on a Sunday. Even when we traveled, he'd always find a church so that we could attend. He also had a unique sense of humor and made everyone happy to be in his company. He loved to play with language. For example, if it were a cold evening, he'd say, using some Spanish, "Put on your *robie of adobe hacienda.*" He'd also ask us the time by saying, "What watch?" We might forget that he was playing with us and respond with the exact time, and then he'd quip, "Such much?" Perhaps, because he was the youngest in the family, his own parents were more relaxed about raising him than they were with his two older sisters, your great-great aunts, Lucille (Lucy) and Eleanor, a green-eyed beauty who later became Sister Mary Angelus, a Franciscan sister, when she was twenty-three.

YOUR GREAT-GRANDFATHER, JOHN SILKE, OKINAWA, 1945

Sister Angelus left the convent in her early fifties after having taught for many years at Cardinal Stritch College near Milwaukee, and earlier serving as principal of a mission school in Waynesville, a mountain town in North Carolina. (There were few Catholics in the Carolinas back then.) I remember that our family picked her up at the convent, where my brother and I saw her without her long black habit for the first time. She had short blonde hair that had a punk rocker look to it because it had been cropped short and uneven. We took our new "Aunt Eleanor" with us to Miami Beach that year and were shocked to see her in a one-piece bathing suit that had cut-outs down each side, which she called her "lattice work."

After Aunt Lucille and her husband, Uncle Martin, moved to Chicago, we'd frequently visit them for the holidays. There's one memory that still moves me when I think about those visits. It might be Christmas Eve. My brother and I would be bundled up against the cold. Dad, wearing his overcoat and Stetson hat, would be in the front seat with my brother, who would have already fallen asleep. From the back seat that I shared with Mom, I'd look out the window at the scattered, snow-covered farm houses on the drive back to Milwaukee. There were warm, inviting lights in those snug houses that made me yearn for my own home and bed. I'd rest my head on Mom's lap. She'd put her arm around me, and I'd fall asleep. In the morning, I'd never remember how I ended up in my own bed.

One of my parents' pleasures, shared with Lucy, her husband Martin, and Eleanor, was going to the horse races during their trips to Florida. They would pool their money and bet on their favorite horses. If they won, they splurged with drinks and dinner at a good restaurant. They were the best of friends and frequently socialized together. It was Aunt Lucy and Uncle Martin who treated my brother and me to trips to New York City on our respective 13th birthdays. They had by then moved to White Plains, NY and wanted to share the Big Apple with us. We visited Rockefeller Center, the Empire State Building, saw the Statue of Liberty, etc. They later did the same for your father and Jana and Pam, Uncle John and Aunt Lana's daughters, your first cousins, once-removed.

Sophie, the tradition Aunt Lucy and Uncle Martin began inspired me to take you to swim with the dolphins in Key Largo to celebrate your thirteenth birthday. And, to celebrate yours, Vincent, we visited John Pennekamp Coral Reef State Park, also in Key Largo. Although we couldn't snorkel because of high seas, we kayaked around the many mangrove islands. I remember that you commented on the clarity of the water and the abundance of sea grasses, saying, "I could do this all day."

# WATER SKIING ON THE AMAZON

*Your father, 13, with his great aunt Lucy, 67, Central Park, NYC, 1981*

Getting back to my father, he frequently used Polish phrases with family, such as *Jak sie masz* (How are you? pronounced Yahk sheh mahsh) and *Dziekwje* (Thank you, pronounced Jen koo yeh). I imagine that he had heard his grandparents speak Polish and these were the only phrases that he remembered. It was common for immigrant parents to encourage their children to learn English as quickly as possible and to speak it at home so they could be perceived as *real* Americans. The down side of this practice was that, rather than becoming bilingual, most children and grandchildren of immigrant parents quickly forgot or never learned the language of their ancestors, becoming monolingual, like most North Americans.

Dad's mother, Barbara Helene, your great-great grandmother, was beautiful, gentle, and kind. I don't remember ever hearing her utter a harsh word. She had lustrous black hair that fell to her waist. I loved to braid it, and, like my dad's, her hair never turned gray. She and her husband, John Michael, after whom Uncle John is named, lived in an attractive apartment on the east side of Milwaukee. There was a fire escape with a little sitting area and view of Lake Michigan at the back of the apartment, where Grandma tended colorful petunias in planters. I remember that she would take me to Bradley Beach, a short walk away. Here is a picture of us seated on a blanket when I'm one-year-old. She wears a big straw hat to protect her fair complexion.

There were two exotic statues that Grandma Silke kept on a small table at the entrance to her apartment. As a small child, those statues of muscular, dark, turbaned men, who might have served a pharaoh in ancient Egypt, seemed huge to me. Grandma said that they were her bodyguards, and that they awakened at night to protect us. Those statues now stand in a *niche* above our fireplace in Pensacola. It's my hope that someone in your family will want them. They're all the physical reminders I have from Barbara Helene.

Grandpa Silke seemed stern to me, although I can't recall him ever being mean. I do remember

AT BRADFORD BEACH, MILWAUKEE, WITH MY PATERNAL GRANDMOTHER, BARBARA HELENE SILKE, 1940. (NOTE THE OLD CARS.)

being afraid, however, of the long black shaving strop that hung from their bathroom sink that he used to sharpen his razor. One fond memory I have of him took place when he was working as a bartender at "The Old South," an upscale cocktail lounge in Milwaukee. I was about four at the time. Dad took me in to greet him. Grandpa Silke seated me on a barstool and delighted me by placing a bowl of Maraschino cherries in front of me, those bright red cherries with the artificial color and preservatives. I remember, too, that he loved to go into the woods to hunt for edible mushrooms. Perhaps this custom came from the Polish traditions with which he grew up. He also loved to fish, so, Vincent, you and he had that in common.

Age five, with my paternal grandfather, John Michael Silke, 1944.

I've tried to find the ship records documenting Grandpa Silke's arrival in the United States, but his, like those pertaining to the arrival of your great-great grandfather Henry Seitz, were lost during World War II. I'm guessing that Grandpa Silke crossed the Atlantic, like Grandpa Seitz, when he was in his late teens or early twenties. Grandma Silke, like Grandma Seitz, was born in Milwaukee, but of Polish-born, not German-born, parents. She and Grandpa Silke were married in 1910. (One of his records states that he was born in Germany; another says he was born in Prussia, because of post-war partitions. Linguistically and culturally, though, he was Polish.)

It still amazes me how much courage early immigrants to this country needed. Most of them would never see their parents again. Certain immigrants (and refugees) to our country still need the same kind of courage. Grandpa Seitz returned to Germany, the "Old Country," only once, in 1915, when his wife Kuni was pregnant with my mother, just before World War I broke out. The story goes that his mother was so excited about seeing him and his family that she had a heart attack at the docks when they were disembarking. To my knowledge, Grandpa Silke never returned to his home across the Atlantic once he reached America. As a mother, I can't imagine the pain my great-great grandparents would have suffered. Most people then didn't have the resources to cross back and forth across the ocean.

I have the gold wedding bands that your great-great grandmothers wore. They are engraved with their initials and those of their spouses along with the dates they wed: Kuni and Henry Seitz in 1907, and John Michael and Barbara Helene in 1910. These rings will belong to your family after my death.

# WATER SKIING ON THE AMAZON

My maternal grandparents (your great-great grandparents), Henry and Kuni Seitz, 50th wedding anniversary, Hartland, Wisconsin, 1957

You'll need to ask your mother about your maternal grandparents, Marian Rose Klein Loesch and Martin Nicholas Loesch, who, unfortunately, died before they had the pleasure of knowing you. (You may not realize it now, but one day you'll understand just how hard it must have been for your then eighteen-year-old mother to have lost her mother to cancer.)

Your mother with your grandparents, Martin Nicholas Loesch and Marian Rose Klein Loesch, Nassau, Bahamas, 1967

You should also ask Papi to fill you in about his parents, Lillian and Wade Taylor, also your great-grandparents.

Papi's mother (your great-grandmother), Lillian Grawin Taylor, 1990s

PAPI'S FATHER (YOUR GREAT-GRANDFATHER),
WADE HAMPTON TAYLOR, 1940S

Uncle John and I were fortunate to have lived near our grandparents while we were growing up. With so much social mobility, few grandparents and grandchildren have regular contact now, so I'm especially grateful for your annual visits to our mountain farmhouse in Montezuma, North Carolina and for the yearly trips we make to see you.

One of my fondest memories as a little girl was spending the night with my mother's parents, grandma and grandpa Seitz, at the beautiful home they built after they had saved all those years, toiling in the bakery. They had a screened-in garden house in the back yard. My girl cousins, Ramona and Karen, who lived in the house behind our grandparents, would come over and we'd play "house" in that sweet garden retreat. In the evening, Grandpa Henry and I would sit at the kitchen table drinking tea and eating smelly Limburger cheese on rye bread. He'd tell me stories, taking a break now and then to say, *Yah, yah, Pahdy* (Patty), with his German accent. Years later, after I graduated from college, he'd introduce me to his friends as his granddaughter, "the speech *terapist*."

Grandma Seitz always had a pot of meat or vegetable stock or soup on the stove because she never threw out any food. Anything left over went into the soup pot. It always tasted good, especially on cold nights. On holidays, Grandma would bring out her best China and crystal, and our big family gathered around the dining room table. Each setting had its own tiny, crystal salt cellar. After dinner, Grandma would play the piano for the adults, while the children played with each other.

## *Things I Wish I Had Not Done*

**MY BROTHER AND I NEVER DOUBTED OUR PARENTS' AND GRANDPARENTS' LOVE FOR US, BUT SOMETIMES MY MOTHER'S LOVE DIDN'T SEEM SO UNCONDITIONAL.** As I grew into adolescence, we had terrible fights, most of them dealing with how I dressed or wore my hair. My agitation all seems so stupid now, but back then I wondered why she needed to meddle in my life, not realizing that she probably saw me as a reflection of herself, of how she raised me, and she wanted me to present my best side to the world. It's just that we had different ideas of what constituted "the best side."

Mom had the tendency to yell when she was angry, and this behavior drove me to my bedroom where I would hide out for hours, or even days, even though I had no computer or Smart phone. My parents became exasperated by all the time I spent alone in my room. I'm sure I was a real pain and thought that I knew everything, at least more than they. I do remember Mom telling me, during one of those angry episodes, that one day I'd understand how much it hurt to have an "ungrateful child." Now I hate that I talked back to her and wish that I had known then what I know now about communication. There's a quote that helps me to be careful about what I say in anger: "Don't say today what you can't take back tomorrow."

My brother agrees that our parents trusted us more than we deserved. Uncle John was a daredevil, and it's amazing that he survived his adolescence. I was generally obedient, being home at night when I should and not testing our parents' generous limits, but I do remember one incident that nearly got me killed and did betray their trust, even though they never learned about it. I was just fifteen and had my learner's permit. My parents were away, and my dad's sleek new Oldsmobile rested in the narrow garage behind our building. I thought I'd surprise my friend Barbara and drive the car to her house and take her for a spin. Nervously, I backed the Oldsmobile out of the garage and down the alley until I could turn around. I crossed busy North Avenue and drove two blocks down Sherman Boulevard. Then I tried to turn right to Barbara's house, but I turned too soon and went over the curb and the lawn of the lady who lived on the corner across from

Barbara's house. The car got hung up on the curb. The lady rushed down the stairs of her house, wildly waving her arms, shouting at me. She took down the car's license number and said she'd be calling my parents and the police. Somehow I got out of there, never visited Barbara, got the car back into the garage, and stayed near the phone for several days. Nothing ever came of it, and my parents died without knowing this story. To this day I don't understand how I had the nerve to attempt something that stupid. I hated the feeling of shame that descended on me for having betrayed my parents' trust.

When thinking of stupid things I've done, I shake my head, amazed at how loony I must have been to have done what comes next: I was spending the night at Barbara's. We were in her bedroom talking about our "boyfriends." They weren't our boyfriends, but we wished they had been. We lightly "carved" their initials into our ankles, like self-inflicted tattoos. We didn't cut deep enough for there to be bleeding, just a bit of a scrape that allowed us to see the letters. Where did we ever come up with that idea?

## *Dating: Attraction, Love, Disappointment, Love*

**I MET AL WHEN I WAS FIFTEEN AND A SOPHOMORE IN HIGH SCHOOL.** He was seventeen, and his parents had just given him permission to join the Marine Corps. Al was half Native-American and very handsome. He didn't have a car, but Dad loaned us his for the evening. Talk about trust! When he took me home, Al gave me my first real kiss, not the spin-the-bottle kind. I was in love for the first time. I moped around, waiting for him to call.

A few months later, after Al had been deployed, I started fainting in chapel and in my classes. I went to our family doctor who pricked my ear, comparing the color of my blood with the colors on a chart that corresponded to hemoglobin levels. Hemoglobin is the oxygen carrying agent in the blood, and if you don't have enough, you become anemic. My blood was orange! I went into the hospital that day. At first, the doctors suspected tuberculosis, and I was kept in isolation. When that was ruled out, a blood specialist thought I might have leukemia. I had to have a painful bone marrow tap before that disorder was ruled out. Finally, the doctors concluded that I had chronic iron deficiency anemia, and I had to have three blood transfusions.

During my long stay in the hospital, I kept waiting for a letter from Al. None was forthcoming, and oh, how I suffered. I had written him a letter from the hospital, giving it to a nurse to mail. In my disappointment, I silently and wrongly blamed the nurse to whom I had given my letter, thinking she had never mailed it.

Years later, there were many boyfriends. In retrospect, I wish I had politely declined most of them. Others I remember fondly, but what's amazing is that, despite having been in love many times, and despite some terrible disappointments associated with those loves, I've overcome wounds I thought I'd live with for the rest of my life, and you will too.

After Al, I didn't date until my senior year, and I never thought I was missing out on anything. For one thing, there were no opportunities to meet boys at my school. Although some of the girls had boyfriends, I don't remember ever feeling embarrassed because I wasn't dating. In my senior year, however, the situation changed because now Barbara and I were going dancing with her older sisters. Great Lakes Naval Station was located in northern Illinois, just a short train ride from Milwaukee, and young sailors on leave would come to Milwaukee and attend the American Legion Post on Sunday afternoons to dance. The Post sat on a bluff high above Lake Michigan and had gorgeous views.

When we were seniors, we became USO hostesses. ("USO" stands for United Services Organization, a non-profit organization that provides services and live entertainment to United States troops and their families.) Fashion called for circle skirts, some decorated with little poodle dogs, worn with one or more crinoline petticoats. When we danced, those skirts would billow out, but all those starched crinolines kept us decent. We cinched our waists with wide belts. No alcohol was served, but there would always be a delicious buffet lunch, and some of Milwaukee's best musicians would provide the big band music. I paid attention to the good dancers, even if they weren't handsome.

The young men who attended those dances came from all over the States. As a rule, they were courteous, well-groomed, and enjoyed having a dancing partner for the afternoon. Although we weren't allowed to leave with the men, sometimes a girl would give her phone number to one she liked, and they would date the next time the sailor had leave. I celebrated my seventeenth birthday at a park overlooking Lake Michigan. My date was Wesley Brown, a sailor from Osage, Wyoming, who presented me with beautiful pearl earrings. Yes, some of the boys we dated would have liked for us to go further than kissing, but a firm "no" was enough to dissuade them.

When I was a college freshman, I was elected Milwaukee's "Miss USO." I wore that high school prom dress again (without the tulle around my shoulders) at the induction ceremony where I received a bouquet of red roses. The next day I threw in the baseball that launched the game of the Milwaukee Braves, a major league team.

**There's No Catch to This!**

Del Crandall, Braves' catcher, welcoming Patricia Silke, 4233 W. North Av., USO queen, to Sunday's ball game. Patricia was chosen by servicemen's votes.

Sentinel photo.

Photo, *The Milwaukee Sentinel*, 1959

## *Choosing a Career Path: The Influence of Family and Environment*

**MOST PARENTS HAVE EXPECTATIONS FOR THEIR CHILDREN, AND THEIR OWN EDUCATIONAL BACKGROUNDS AND SOCIO-ECONOMIC CLASS INFLUENCE THOSE EXPECTATIONS.** Most parents want their children to succeed in life, to get good educations, to make a decent wage, and to live productive, contented lives. After World War II, and the pressure to support their families, most married men were happy to find a decent job. My father found work selling shoes at a store a few blocks from home. I remember it had an X-Ray machine into which we peered to see if there was enough room in the new shoe for swiftly growing toes. As if the machine were a toy, we went back repeatedly to see those wiggling appendages against an eerie green light. No one considered the danger from radiation.

Later, Dad had a friend who helped land him a job with Graf's Soda Company. He did well, especially when the first A& P super market opened and others followed. Graf's soda was popular, and "Grandpa Graf's Creamy-Top Root Beer" was especially popular. The more Dad sold, the higher his paycheck because his salary was based on commissions. During periods when sales were depressed, so were his paychecks, a source of stress on payday in our household. Gradually, Dad was promoted to district manager, then to overall sales manager, the job he held when he died of a heart attack in 1977, at age sixty-one, three years after my mother's death (more on her death later).

Although my parents hadn't attended college, they always assumed my brother and I would get university degrees. Like your dad, my father was always available to help me with my school assignments. He especially loved those involving the writing of essays and compositions. His education at Cathedral High School had been excellent. There he studied his Catholic religion, Latin, English, literature, history, math, and music. (Throughout high school he also continued to serve as an "altar boy" at St. John's Cathedral.)

Mom attended beautician school after graduating from Milwaukee's Holy Angels Academy, but she only worked for a short time in that field. She enjoyed working in her parents' bakery where she was well-liked because of her outgoing personality. It was Mom who taught me how to give change when I started working part-time in the bakery. Giving customers the correct change sounds easy now, with calculators built into computerized cash registers, but then you had to know how to quickly calculate because no cash register told you how much change the customer was due. That skill came in handy when I later took a part-time job at Farber's Drug Store, just down the block.

My favorite job was making sundaes and milk shakes behind the soda fountain. But what was I going to do with the rest of my life? Fortunately, my friend Barbara's sisters had college degrees and often spoke of their professions, so I listened carefully as they described their jobs. Cathy was a nurse, and it was she who helped me when I was in the hospital with that blood disorder. As part of the diagnosis, I had to swallow a tube that was inserted through my nose in order to retrieve gastric liquid from my stomach. It was a horrible procedure. I kept gagging until Cathy calmed me and inserted the tube in a way that helped me swallow it. Maybe it was her patient and caring act that influenced me to consider nursing.

Marlene, another of Barbara's sisters, was a speech therapist. She worked with children who had speech disorders that might have been caused by cleft palate, mental retardation, autism, cerebral palsy, or stuttering. Other children simply had articulation problems. Marlene also worked with hearing impaired children who had trouble speaking because they couldn't properly hear themselves or others. She tested their hearing and, if they had deficits, she referred them to specialists who might fit the children with hearing aids. She also taught them how to use their residual hearing to speak as well as possible.

In the end, I decided in favor of speech therapy and audiology and completed a rigorous four-year program at Marquette University, where I earned my Bachelor of Science degree. But something happened during that last year of college that will surprise you.

## *Semper Fi, Always Faithful: Your Grandmother Joins the Marine Corps*

**WHEN I STARTED THIS MEMOIR, I DECIDED NOT TO SHARE THE NEXT STORY WITH YOU BECAUSE IT STILL EMBARRASSES ME.** I've chosen to reveal it, however, because it's a perfect illustration of how easy it is for a young person to be attracted by what, at first appearances, seems glamorous. At the beginning of my senior year in college, I noticed two very handsome Marine Corps recruiters in the student union, where I went every day for lunch. They looked very smart wearing their "dress blues." Catching me staring at them, they smiled and beckoned me over to their display table. They told me how many adventures I'd have if I were to join the Corps. With a college degree, I would qualify for Officers' Candidate School, and soon I'd be on my way to an exciting career. A few days later, I had my hand up in the air and was sworn into the Marine Corps, ready to see the world.

Had I believed that I could practice as a speech therapist in the Marine Corps? What did those men tell me that persuaded me to make such a radical decision? After four years of college, maybe I was still unsure about my career choice. Joining the Marine Corps would have been an honorable decision, but what might have been less honorable was my impulsive behavior.

My parents were distressed. "What were you thinking?" they asked. It's not that they would not have been proud of me. After all, Dad was a proud veteran. They must have seen that I wasn't thinking clearly if I could be so easily side-tracked. Before graduation, my parents encouraged me to seek a one-year deferment that would give me an opportunity to practice my profession before reporting for duty. The Marine Corps agreed. Now I had to find a job in my field. I took one as the only speech therapist in rural Rock County, Wisconsin, near the Illinois border, about three hours southwest of Milwaukee by car. Right after signing the contract, I received a job offer from St. Thomas in the Virgin Islands.

## *First Job: So This Is What All That Education Is About*

**EXCEPT FOR TWO SUMMERS AT GIRL SCOUT CAMP, I LEFT HOME FOR THE FIRST TIME IN AUGUST, 1961 AT AGE TWENTY-TWO.** Mom helped me find a place to live, a small garage apartment behind a farmhouse in the country near Janesville, the county seat. The apartment was cozy with only two rooms and a bath. There were deep woods on two sides. I slept on a sofa-bed in the living room. Being a city girl, I wasn't used to the complete darkness at night and to the noises that would *clunk* and *thunk* while I was trying to sleep. Was some bad guy coming to get me? One night I got a butcher knife and hid in the kitchen, waiting for the intruder to enter. In the morning I discovered that chestnuts falling on my roof caused the noises. At Christmas, I put on my boots and warm clothes, took my butcher knife again, and went into the snow-covered woods where I cut down a small fir tree and dragged it home, like I had seen people do in movies.

Being the only speech therapist in a large rural county, I visited every school, and most of them had only one classroom where a single teacher taught all the grades. I screened the children for speech, language, and hearing disorders, and I did it in closets, corridors, a teacher's small office, or in "cloak rooms," an old-fashioned term referring to a long room with hooks on the walls where children hung their coats and left their boots on rainy or snowy days. There were a few times when my 1957 yellow and black Plymouth ended up in a ditch, but a helpful farmer would always give me a tow. Eventually, the County added another therapist and we shared the student load.

## *The Peace Corps: "The Toughest Job You'll Ever Love"*

**IN 1961, THE SAME YEAR I GRADUATED FROM MARQUETTE UNIVERSITY, PRESIDENT JOHN F.** Kennedy introduced to the public the idea of a Peace Corps. His words, "Ask not what your country can do for you, but what you can do for your country," have become famous and certainly influenced me. He envisioned a corps of volunteers of all ages who would serve for two years in poor countries throughout the world. They would live among the people and work with them to improve their social, health, and economic conditions. The people in these countries would get to know Americans by coming in contact with ordinary citizens. The volunteers would present a different face to those who had only known America through its government's policies, some of which had not been popular. I really wanted to be one of those first Peace Corps volunteers but how could I when I had a commitment to the Marine Corps?

I applied to the Peace Corps anyway, just to see if I'd be accepted. Who was this girl I'm now writing about? Who were the other applicants who would risk joining a new government organization and take two years out of their lives to work under difficult circumstances in poor countries? If I were accepted, where would I be sent? Could I stand to be away from my family for two years? I wanted to travel and thought a country in Latin America would be perfect, giving me a chance to practice the Spanish I had studied in high school and college.

In spring, 1962, I received a telegram from Sargent Shriver, then director of the Peace Corps and brother-in-law to President Kennedy, notifying me that I had been accepted. If I signed on, I would have two months of academic training at Cornel University in Ithaca, New York and one month of physical training in Puerto Rico before heading to Peru. Now there was just one obstacle: How did I get out of the Marine Corps? I wrote a letter pleading with them to release me because I had found another way to serve. Once again, they obliged me with an "honorable discharge." I remember my mother's first reaction when it had all been sorted out: "But Patty, Peru's so far away," she said.

At Cornell I met the other 101 trainees. Some were as young as eighteen; a few were in their mid sixties. I'm still friends with Sandy, with whom I shared a large dorm room in an old, ivy-covered building. In addition to intense Spanish language instruction, we also studied the history of American Democracy, the history of Communism, then considered a threat in Latin America, and the history and culture of Peru. Those trainees who were already bi-lingual in Spanish and English studied Quechua, one of the primary languages of the Andean people. Not knowing what part of Peru we were headed to, the Amazon, high Andes, or coastal dessert, we also had to take classes that would help us survive wherever we were sent. We learned first aid (in case there were no doctors); food preservation (no refrigerators); equitation (no public transport but horses), and the slaughtering and butchering of animals (no meat available in stores).

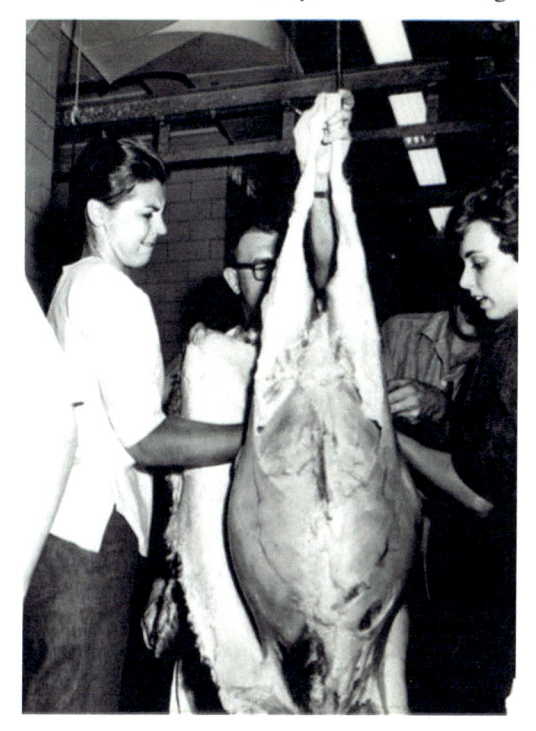

AT LEFT, SKINNING A SHEEP, PEACE CORPS TRAINING, CORNELL UNIVERSITY, 1962

We usually had Sundays free when we'd go to a waterfall on campus that had a natural stone waterslide that dumped us into a pool of icy water. We also enjoyed picnics and sing-alongs. Folk music was big, and a few of the volunteers played guitar. Friendships developed and some young men and women fell in love only to have the relationships break up once they arrived in Peru.

In Puerto Rico, the emphasis changed to the development of our physical endurance skills. In addition to long runs on muddy trails in the rain forest, we learned survival swimming in a pool and later in the Caribbean Sea, where we had to remove garage mechanic overalls (bathing suits underneath) and make them into life preservers by blowing up the legs and sleeves, all the while treading water in heavy surf.

We also learned mountaineering techniques by ascending a jagged cliff. The only way down was to rappel, to descend, out and around a scary overhang, using a double rope that had been secured around a rock from above and strategically wrapped around our butts. You lowered yourself by gradually letting out that rope with your hand while using your feet and legs to bounce back off the cliff as you descended. Sandy and I prayed for rain before it was our turn so that the activity would be cancelled. No such luck.

I was most afraid when I had to rappel down the side of a monstrous dam in the interior of the island. Seeing a sixty-five-year-old grandmother successfully rappel that dam, gave me courage. We also learned topographic map-reading skills, how to find our way from one point on the island to another using a map that only indicated mountain heights and depths of valleys, a map on which no town was identified. We even had to spend a night alone in the heart of the rain forest. After inspecting for tarantulas, I spent the night under a rock overhang after first cutting down banana leaves to cover the ground. It was tough building a fire to cook dehydrated soup because the fuel was wet.

There was a public health component in our training. I was assigned to a small group who had to take samples of fecal material from outhouses in remote areas to be delivered to the health department where it would be tested for parasites. Because they thought my Spanish better than theirs, the other members in my group charged me with introducing our task to the people who lived in the isolated houses we visited. Think of how strange it would be if someone came to your door and asked to take a sample of fecal material from your toilet. Despite the bizarre intrusion, most of the people gave us permission. We used long sticks with swabs at the end to collect the samples. Then we placed the swabs in test tubes. We referred to this duty as "honey dipping."

ANDEANS DURING CARNIVAL (PHOTO TAKEN THROUGH TRAIN WINDOW), CUZCO, PERU, 1963

## *Peru: The Belly Button of the World*

**AFTER A BRIEF VISIT WITH MY FAMILY IN MILWAUKEE, I JOINED EIGHTY-ONE OTHER VOLUNTEERS WHO HAD NOT BEEN "DESELECTED" FOR AN OVER-NIGHT PAN AMERICAN FLIGHT FROM MIAMI TO LIMA.** We arrived at dawn, bleary-eyed, yet expectant. The Peace Corps put us up for a week at the Alcazar Hotel in downtown Lima. There we received additional orientation to the country, lots of vaccinations, and more health warnings. Never drink the water unless you've boiled it for twenty minutes, and never eat fruits and vegetables unless they can be peeled or soaked in an iodine solution, advice that we could not always take without offending our Peruvian hosts.

To what part of Peru would we be sent? And would we be with the friends we had made during training? Alas, my Cornell room-mate, Sandy, was sent to Piura in the far north of that 3,440-mile-long country, and I was sent to Arequipa, in the far south.

Forty-two of us boarded a chartered school bus and traveled down the Pan-American Highway that hugged the rugged Pacific coast. Towering sand dunes lined the east side of the highway. I stared at the magnificent surf and at the seabirds swarming above the western rocky shoreline, recalling that *guano,* the birds' excrement, was scraped off those rocks to be used as fertilizer, a valuable export for the country. A few hours south of Lima, we were delayed for several hours because an avalanche of sand covered the highway. After a bulldozer operator had cleared the highway, and, as night fell, we headed inland, over the dark, foreboding Andes.

We were entering the world of the ancient Incas, whose ancestors were said to have emerged from Lake Titicaca, the highest navigable lake in the world. (Four years later, I would spend an entire summer near its shores while engaged to Papi.) According to legend, Inca, Manco Capac, and his sister/wife, Mama Ocllo, emerged from the lake with orders from the Sun God, Viracocha. According to the god's commands, the two were to populate the land. Manco Capac carried a gold staff, and when it finally sank into fertile ground, he was to establish the kingdom of Cuzco, the umbilicus of the world, the "belly button" from which civilization would spread.

PEACE CORPS VOLUNTEERS ARE STRANDED ON THE PAN-AMERICAN
HIGHWAY AFTER A SAND SLIDE, 1962. THAT'S ME IN THE WHITE DRESS.
(CUSTOMS CALLED FOR WOMEN TO WEAR DRESSES OR SKIRTS.)

We arrived in Arequipa, dirty and disheveled. This was the exact moment in which I met your future grandfather. He helped me off the bus in our new neighborhood of Alto de Selva Alegre, "Height of the Happy Forest." His Peace Corps group had been scheduled to arrive a month before ours, but Peru had undergone a military coups, so to avoid any potential harm to the volunteers, your grandfather's group was held back in the States until order had been restored in the country.

"Alto," as we used to call it, was an enormous *barriada*, a poor neighborhood that perched on the lower slopes of *Misti*, the snow-capped volcano that reaches 19,101 feet. All of Arequipa lies in an active earthquake zone, and the city has been destroyed several times by major quakes. In fact, at this writing on July 22, 2014, during the last three months, the Department of Arequipa has known ten earthquakes under 5.5 magnitude. Whenever there was a tremor, when the ground trembled underneath our feet, we would rush out of our little houses and join the Peruvian residents who were anxiously looking up at the volcano for the telltale wisps of smoke that signaled activity. (Both of you have already seen those smoky wisps from the Arenal volcano in Costa Rica, when we traveled there as a family in 2013.)

# WATER SKIING ON THE AMAZON

Most of the people who lived in Alto were *Mestizo*, of Indian and Spanish descent, although some were entirely indigenous, descendants of the Incas, and they spoke their native Quechua. The *barriadas* in Peru developed over time, as people from the high sierra descended to the coastal cities to find jobs and better living conditions. *Barriadas* are now called *pueblos jóvenes* or "young towns" in Peru, and the squatters who seem to descend overnight are called *paracaidistas*, parachutists.

You could tell how long a family had been in Alto by the size and quality of their houses. Someone newly arrived might have only a house made of tin, propped up by large stones. The roof would also be tin, with boulders resting on top to secure it. Other houses were made of *sillar*, white volcanic stone that had steel rods reinforcing the construction. Some even had a rudimentary second floor. Granddaddy Joe and I returned to Peru in 1995 to visit the places where I had lived and worked, in preparation for the writing of my novel inspired by those two years. I was pleasantly surprised to see that Alto had been transformed into an attractive, low middle-class neighborhood with electricity and piped in water.

Then, however, there was only one *bodega*, a tiny store that offered a few bars of soap, cooking oil, warm beer, beans, rice, and a few other staples. We had no cars and relied on crowded public busses to take us to town where shops offered some of the specialty items that we were used to, like peanut butter. One of the more enterprising volunteers figured out how to make her own peanut butter and earned a little money by selling it to volunteers. I missed fresh milk. The only milk we had came in powder or cans.

For several weeks the women volunteers lived in a classroom in a newly built school house, with cots lined up against the walls. But there were flush toilets and a few cold-water showers in the bathroom. We were there during the Cuban Missile Crisis, huddled around my short-wave radio, wondering if we'd ever see our families again. The Soviets had placed missiles in Cuba, pointed at the United States. President Kennedy issued an ultimatum: There would be war unless the missiles were removed. We received orders that we could not leave the school. Peruvian university students held anti-United States protests in the central plaza. At night we heard cars screech by our school. In the morning there were anti-U.S. signs on the school door.

The Soviets backed down and withdrew their missiles. President Kennedy remained our hero, and, we were eager to begin our work in Peru. Although the school provided temporary shelter, we now had to find our own accommodations.

Carol, a young volunteer from Miami, and I found a one-room house, made from *sillar*, not far from the school. We divided it with a curtain to make a kitchen and a bedroom where we could put our Peace Corps-issued cots with thin mattresses. We made curtains for the window in the bedroom and made a couch from *sillar* blocks with pillows on top. (I hid the dollar bills my mother sent with her letters between the blocks.)

When our little place was presentable, we had a house-warming party and invited the volunteers who lived in our area. I had brought a battery-operated phonograph from the States and several records in the one large travel trunk the Peace Corps shipped for us. We served Peruvian rum mixed with Inca Kola, and celebrated the beginning of our lives in Peru. I remember that Papi, your future grandfather, and I danced the jitterbug at that party. We remained friends even after his early departure from the Peace Corps so that he could finish his studies at George Washington University. He did what was right for him. Many of us struggled to find worthwhile work while we were in Peru. Unlike promises made to us, there were no positions we could simply walk into. Many of us started projects that for any number of reasons failed, and many volunteers were frustrated, feeling their skills were not being employed. The Peace Corps, now fifty-three years-old, has learned a lot since then and has succeeded, for the most part, in correcting early errors.

Getting back to our house, we were lucky to have a "modern" latrine in the backyard. It had a toilet bowl over a hole in the ground, so you could sit down. We had to keep a bucket of water from the cistern next to the toilet for flushing. It also had a low privacy fence that wasn't good for tall girls like me, and there was no door. The landlord was fattening a vicious turkey in his yard, and we had to wield a broom against it whenever we used the latrine. It was common for all of us to have dysentery now and then. You feel as though your guts are going to spill out, and not having a bathroom in your house makes things worse. I never take indoor plumbing for granted now, and every time I take a shower I give thanks for clean water, especially hot water.

# WATER SKIING ON THE AMAZON

The cistern collected water during the rainy season that could be used for washing clothes. We got our drinking, cooking, and bathing water, however, from a tank truck that came to our *barriada* once a week. We would line up, buckets in hand, with our neighbors. Even though the water came from the city of Arequipa, we still had to boil it before drinking. To bathe we used two basins of water, one for soaping our bodies, the other for rinsing. We did our hair the same way. If more people in the United States understood what a precious resource water is, they would be hesitant to waste it.

With my neighbors on water day in Alto de Selva Alegre, 1962. Women volunteers often wore scarves because of the dust, and the sunglasses were essential against the glare. (Note the water truck and housing in the background.)

We cooked on a Primus stove that had to be pumped a magical number of times before the kerosene in its small tank would ignite the burner that had been preheated with alcohol. It had only one burner that was sufficient for heating water for instant coffee or canned soup, if we could find any. I remember cooking canned corned beef on one side of a pan with canned peaches on the other. It was surprisingly tasty. Given the inconvenience of going to the market daily, added to the time involved in food preparation, it was easier to eat at the Mogambo, an inexpensive restaurant in downtown Arequipa where the volunteers frequently gathered, and the friendly waiters put up with our emerging Spanish. One of our favorite dishes, especially when we had just received our living allowance of $90.00 per month, was *lomo montado*, a tender piece of beef "mounted" with a fried egg, served with *papas fritas*, French fries. The people in the *barriadas* rarely ate beef and would never have been able to afford a meal in a restaurant. More typically, if there were meat in a meal, it would be goat or guinea pig, both of which are tasty, especially roasted.

The director of the Peace Corps in Peru didn't want us to accept invitations to eat at the houses of wealthy Peruvians. We were supposed to live and work with the poor. In his mind, it would be contrary to the Peace Corp's mission to associate with the rich. At one of our assemblies, I stood up and asked the director how the gap between the rich and poor could be bridged if the rich had no understanding of how the poor lived or why we were even there. The volunteers applauded, but the director was put off by my question, and, from that time on, he thought of me as a trouble-maker. Meanwhile, he lived in very comfortable surroundings.

Many of us were told that we'd be able to practice the professions for which we had studied in the States, but that promise proved to be unrealistic. The needs of the people were too basic. Rather than working with speech impaired children, for example, I helped to set up a pre-school in a neighboring *barriada* called Chapi Chico. The children spoke only Quechua, and we would teach them in basic Spanish. One day on my way to our little tin school house, I was chased by a pack of wild dogs. I called for help and threw stones at the dogs until the women came out of their houses and chased them away.

# WATER SKIING ON THE AMAZON

CHILDREN WITH TYPICAL HOUSING IN CHAPI CHICO, NEAR AREQUIPA, 1962. (NOTE THE ABSENCE OF ANYTHING GREEN, AND THAT ONE CHILD WEARS SHOES; THE OTHER DOESN'T).

PATRICIA S. TAYLOR EDMISTEN

WITH ANOTHER VOLUNTEER AND PRE-SCHOOL CHILDREN IN FRONT OF A SHRINE IN CHAPI CHICO, 1962. (NOTE THAT ONLY TWO CHILDREN WEAR SHOES ON THE ROCKY TERRAIN.)

WITH SANDY IN FRONT OF THE CATHEDRAL, PLAZA DE ARMAS, AREQUIPA, PERU, 1963

During the summer (December-March), the volunteers established a camp on a sandy beach near the city of Mollendo. A train took a different group of children from Arequipa every week. The girls slept on cots on top of the sand in a huge tent borrowed from the Peruvian Army, the boys in another. We ate under another large tent, and women from the town cooked for us. They served us corn meal mush every morning, topped with a big lump of hard brown sugar. We bathed the children in a cold water spring that gushed from the cliff behind our encampment. Although the beach was just a few hours from Arequipa, none of the children had ever seen the ocean; most had never left their *barriadas*. They played in the ocean every day. We volunteers stationed ourselves in waist-high water, facing the campers, so we could see if any had difficulty in the cold, choppy water. (At that latitude, even though it was summer, the Humboldt Current that flows north from the southern tip of Chile to northern Peru, keeps the Pacific cold year-round.) To raise money for the camp, we operated a snack bar called *Hot Dogs Tio Sam* (Uncle Sam's Hot Dogs). A banner with a flag and an image of Uncle Sam flew above our enterprise.

On one Sunday, between the departure of one group of children and the arrival of another, the volunteers planned a picnic on a Sunday afternoon at a small rocky beach. I was swimming when a sea lion emerged right next to me. It had to have been a male because it was enormous. I swam like crazy to get away, but he didn't pursue me, probably more afraid of me than I of him.

# WATER SKIING ON THE AMAZON

## *Ica, Peru: the Flood*

**IN SPRING, 1963, THERE WAS A DEVASTATING FLOOD IN ICA, A CITY NOT FAR FROM THE PACIFIC OCEAN.** The snow melt from the Andes was so great it caused the rivers that ran to the sea to overflow their banks. In Ica, the man who operated the dikes that would have allowed the water to overflow onto cotton crops decided not to open them to protect the investments of the rich land owners. As a result, the river water invaded the *barriadas* of the poor. Their reed and mud houses along the banks of the river washed away; many people died; many were injured, and many more got sick from waterborne diseases. I was among fifteen volunteers sent to do relief work. When we first arrived, we shoveled mud and debris along with the people. Suspicious of us at first, by the evening of the second day, the women somehow managed to cook a generous meal of rice and beans for us, and the men brought out the *pisco*, a clear grape brandy famous to that area. We had been accepted.

During the next few weeks, I joined forces with Ruth, who had worked as a licensed practical nurse in the States before joining the Peace Corps. The two of us began a medical clinic in a small storehouse loaned to us by Caritas, the Catholic relief organization. It was located on the river bed that, by then, was dry and swarming with flies because the people used it as a latrine. Ruth spoke little Spanish, so I translated for her. Neither of us, however, spoke Quechua, so we found a twelve-year-old girl named Magda who was fluent in Spanish and Quechua but didn't speak English. The three of us cleaned out the warehouse, killed the flies, begged for first aid supplies from the Peace Corps, and started seeing patients.

Although I had no medical training, I did know the basics about public health, first aid, and the disease cycle. Many of the children we saw were malnourished, and, as a result, they were more vulnerable to ordinary childhood diseases. What we would consider an ordinary cold in the U.S., might put a child at risk for dying. Gradually, we were able to provide rehydration salts for children with dysentery, food supplements, vitamins, inoculations, and antibiotics. Later, a medical doctor from the only hospital in Ica joined us a few hours every week. Several months after my arrival, I was overjoyed when my friend Sandy transferred to Ica and joined us in the clinic.

WITH OUR ASSISTANT MAGDA, AFTER THE FLOOD, ICA, 1963. (NOTE THE REED AND MUD HOUSING LOCATED ALONG THE RIVER BED.)

AFTER THE FLOOD, ICA, 1963

One afternoon a young girl, no more than nine, brought her baby sister, to the clinic. Baby Celinda had been crawling on the floor and tipped over a kettle of boiling water. Burns covered her body. I did what I could before carrying her through a crowded market to the hospital a long distance away. She needed to have a godmother, someone to vouch for her at the hospital, so I held Celinda while a priest baptized her in the hospital chapel. The baby later died of her burns. For many years after her death I asked myself if there was something more I could have done to save her.

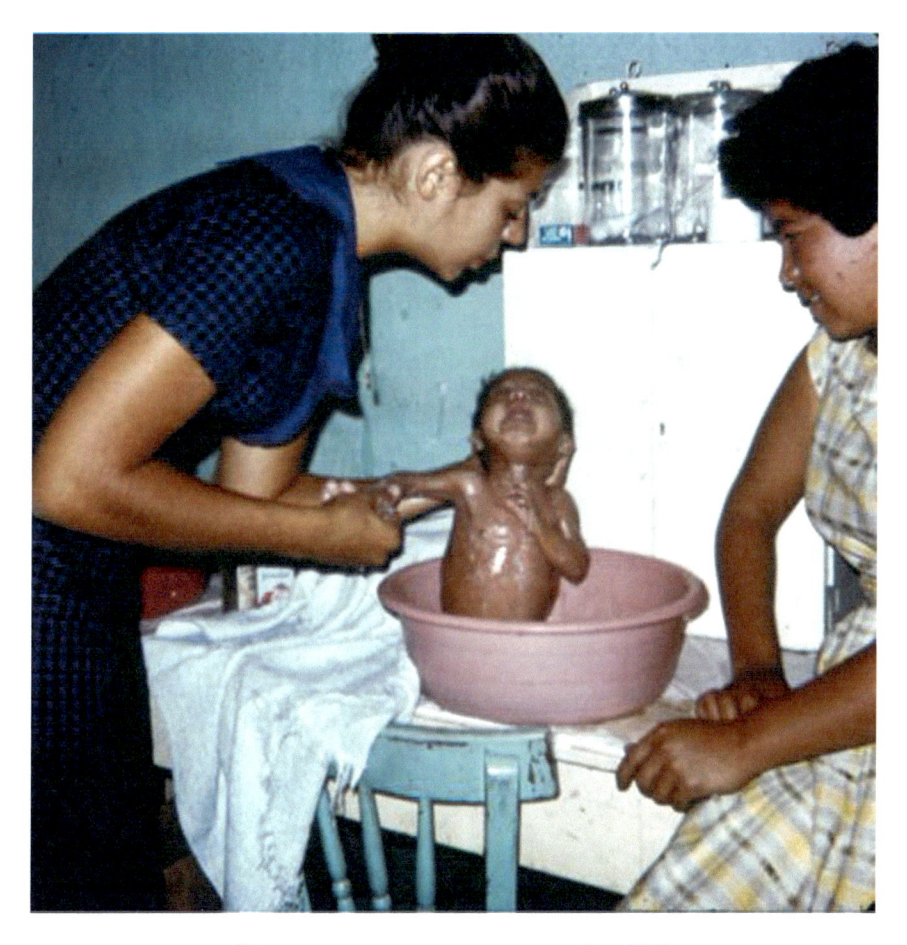

WASHING A MALNOURISHED BABY, ICA, 1963

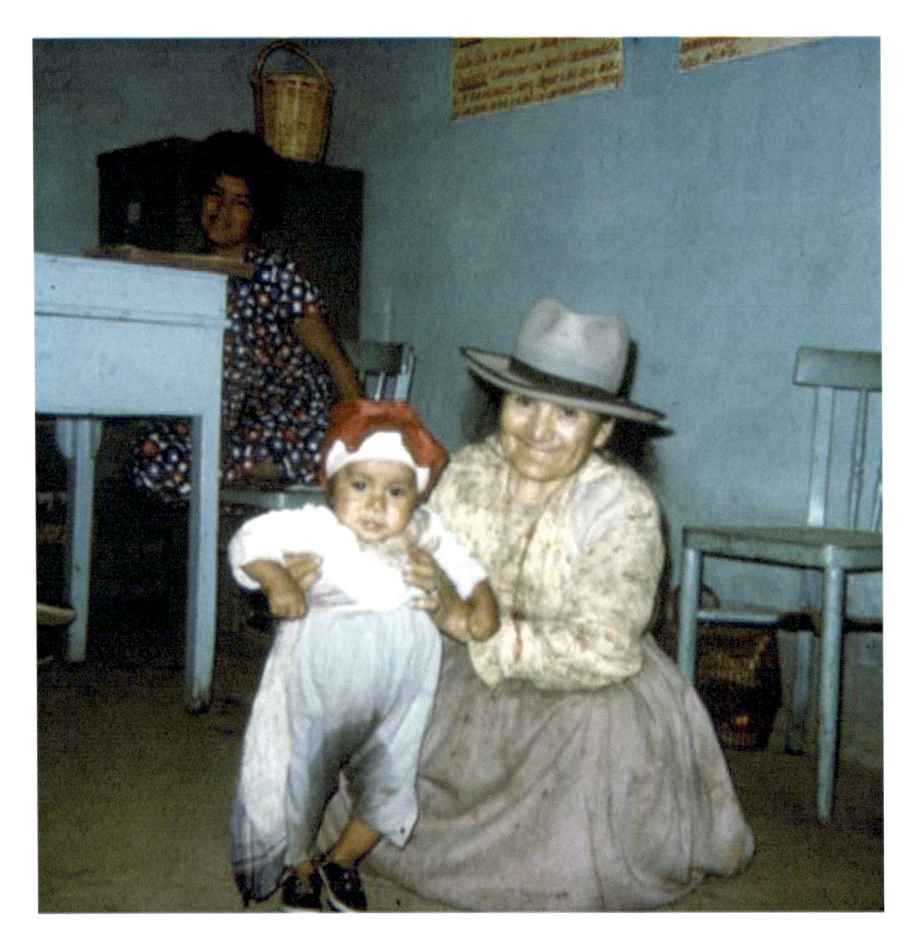

MAGDA, IN THE CLINIC WITH A WET BABY BOY AND HIS
QUECHUA-SPEAKING GRANDMOTHER, ICA, 1963

In Ica I lived with Mary Ann, a volunteer from Delaware who worked at the credit cooperative that Caritas operated. I was grateful that she took me in because her housing was a great improvement over what I had been used to in Arequipa. Mary Ann had cold running water in the rustic kitchen and an inside bathroom with a cold water shower that wet every surface. There was a bar-covered, four-foot by four-foot opening in the roof between our bedroom and the kitchen and bath area. The chickens that lived on the roof couldn't fall through into our house because of the bars, but their feathers floated down, and their poop plopped. Sandy moved in with us when she arrived in Ica to help with the flood relief efforts.

# *Peru Mourns: President John F. Kennedy's Assassination*

**ON THE EVENING OF NOVEMBER 22, 1963, MY FRIENDS AND I WERE LEAVING THE REX MOVIE THEATER IN DOWNTOWN ICA WHEN WE SAW A CHALKBOARD SET UP ON THE SIDEWALK.** The people exiting the theater were swarming around it. We nudged closer and saw the words in Spanish that read, "President Kennedy killed by bullet." Before we could grasp the situation, many Peruvians began to embrace us, knowing we represented e*l Cuerpo de Paz,* "the Peace Corps." Some referred to us as "Kennedy's Children." We were in a state of shock, wondering if such awful news could be true. Businesses closed the next morning. Many had black wreaths on their doors as a sign of mourning. In fact, a Peruvian hung such a wreath on the door of the medical clinic. The sign over the door now read, *Posta Médica John F. Kennedy.*

WITH VOLUNTEERS NORMA, SANDY, AND FRIENDS, NEAR THE MEDICAL CLINIC, ICA, 1963

## Water Skiing on the Amazon

**THE PEACE CORPS WASN'T ALL WORK AND NO PLAY.** Occasionally, we'd take a *collectivo*, a shared taxi, to Lima where we'd stay at the Alcazar Hotel and soak in a hot tub. While in Lima, we'd go to *Todos*, a restaurant in the upscale suburb of Miraflores, where we'd order cheeseburgers and a milk shake or a hot fudge sundae.

On three occasions, I used my accrued leave time to travel to distant locations in Latin America. On my first journey, I flew through a maze of towering, snow-covered peaks that seemed so close I might have touched them if the window had been open. The passengers sucked on oxygen in the small propeller plane headed to Iquitos, a frontier-like town in northeast Peru. Iquitos lies at the juncture of the rivers that merge to become the mighty Amazon, after the Nile, the second longest river in the world.

Men dressed in khaki walked about with anacondas over their necks; others sold colorful blue and yellow McCaw's. It was hot, sultry, and had an air of danger about it. I stayed at the National Tourist Hotel, the only decent lodging in town. The next day I explored a few dark, narrow tributaries in a dugout canoe, amazed at the gigantic water lily pads, the *Victoria amazonica*, that can be three meters wide, with lovely white flowers that turn pink. I also learned about a water ski club that offered rides on one of the Amazon's main tributaries, *The Rio Negro*. I had learned to ski on calm Beaver Lake in Wisconsin, where relatives had a home, but the fish there were innocent perch and blue gill, not flesh-eating piranhas. I wouldn't risk it now, but back then the challenge appealed to me. Pride does go before a fall, and I fell. The driver of the boat turned around, followed me downstream, and picked me up before I was swept away in the rapidly flowing river that resembled *café con leche*.

A year later, after saving money from our Peace Corps allowance, and with help from my parents, I flew to Rio de Janeiro and visited Copacabana, where Papi and I later lived when your dad was a baby. I saw the immense statue of Christ on the mountain called *Corcovado*. From Rio I flew to São Paulo and from there by small plane to Iguaçu Falls, one of the most breathtaking sights in the world. The falls cover 1.7 miles and separate Argentina and Brazil. I stayed at the old *Hotel das Cataratas* on the Brazilian side and remember taking a pretty path through the rain forest to the falls. Brilliant butterflies lighted on my arms and head on the way down to the falls. On that same trip I visited Montevideo and Punta del Este, Uruguay.

A few months before we returned to the States, Sandy and I took a *collectivo* from Ica to Tacna, the southernmost city in Peru. There we crossed the border and caught a plane in Arica, Chile that took us south to Santiago, the capital. We flew over the long Atacama desert that stretches six hundred miles along the Pacific coast. The desert is said to be the driest place in the world.

STANDING IN DOORWAY OF AN INCA RUIN, AGE TWENTY-FOUR, PISAC, 1963

PATRICIA S. TAYLOR EDMISTEN

With my parents at the Milwaukee airport the
day of my return from Peru, June, 1964

# *A Pain in the Butt: The Influence of the Peace Corps on My Life*

**THERE WAS NO GREATER FORMATIVE EXPERIENCE IN MY LIFE THAN THE TWO YEARS I SPENT IN THE PEACE CORPS.** I left the culture I knew and entered another so rich and exotic that it would take me nearly a year to feel at home. Without family, we relied strongly upon our North American and Peruvian friends, some of whom remain my friends to this day. In time, perhaps, you will read my novel, *The Mourning of Angels,* inspired by those two years. It is historically set, and people who have read it say they feel as though they have been transported to Peru. A few years ago I wrote *Body of Peace,* the screenplay based on the book, using for the title the literal English translation of *Cuerpo de Paz,* (Peace Corps).

Actual volunteers and Peruvians I knew influenced my portrayal of certain characters in the book. Rafael, the male protagonist, for example, has traits I admire in men I've known, but I invented his character. Lydia, the female protagonist, experiences much of what I lived in Peru, but she confronts more dangerous circumstances than I faced, although I had many close calls. When the book came out, I was deluged with questions from former Peace Corps volunteers about who was who in the book. Others asked if I "really had a baby in Peru." I didn't, but it's common for people to forget they're reading a novel, and maybe that's as it should be.

It was difficult returning to family life after my return. I was overcome with guilt when I opened the refrigerator door and saw that it had been stocked with goodies in my honor, along with the staples I had missed like cold milk, cheeses, cold cuts, butter, fruit, and vegetables. There was ice cream in the freezer. Mom would shop once a week for groceries, and food would stay fresh until she shopped again. In Peru, we had no refrigeration and shopped daily at an outdoor market. Of all the luxuries, however, the biggest turned out to be our bathtub, shower, and hot water. Oh, and drinking water straight from the tap.

I found that I had little in common with average North Americans, with their emphasis on the latest cars, fashion, and appliances. I judged their complaints to be superficial, and I became impatient, intolerant, and one big pain in the butt. I later learned that most returning volunteers experienced the same sense of displacement. It took a long time to adjust, more time than it took me to adjust to life in Peru.

I no longer saw the United States as the center of the universe. I loved my country more than ever, but I learned that its foreign policies could be wrong and even harmful. I wanted to be part of the solution to poverty, wanted to help foster understanding of what caused malnutrition. To do that I would need to go back to school, but I found myself unable to study what I wanted because I lacked the money. Universities were just beginning to offer financial assistance to returning Peace Corps volunteers, but there were just a few scholarships for us, unlike today.

That said, even though I wasn't able to earn a Master's degree in political science, Latin American studies, or foreign languages, I did get a graduate assistantship because of my Peace Corps service. It came from the Office of International Education at the University of Wisconsin-Milwaukee. Although I didn't study in the discipline that most matched my new interests, the values that evolved during those two years in the Peace Corps have influenced the way I lived and continue to live—my friendships, political affiliation, charities, the courses I later taught, how I taught them, and, most importantly, the way I raised your father.

Among the six books I've written, only one, *The Treasures of Pensacola Beach,* was not borne out of a passion for social justice. *Nicaragua Divided: La Prensa and the Chamorro Legacy; The Autobiography of María Elena Moyano: The Life and Death of a Peruvian Activist; The Mourning of Angels; Wild Women with Tender Hearts,* (that won a Peace Corps Writers Award), and *A Longing for Wisdom: One Woman's Conscience and her Church,* were products of that passion.

## *Graduate Study Followed by Marriage to Papi*

**THE GRADUATE ASSISTANTSHIP I RECEIVED FROM THE UNIVERSITY OF WISCONSIN AT MILWAUKEE REQUIRED THAT I TEACH AS WELL AS GO TO SCHOOL.** I taught English to Venezuelan students who were working on their Master's degrees in counseling psychology. As for my studies, I lucked out and had a rigorous training program in language and learning disorders in children.

During my graduate program, I happened to attend an informal reunion of returned Peace Corps volunteers in Washington, D.C. who had served in Arequipa, Peru. At a party I ran into your future grandfather, whom I had not seen in a few years. He was finishing his Bachelor's degree at George Washington University. The next day we visited a few museums and had lunch. That brief interlude led to a flurry of letters between us. Meanwhile, in Jan., 1966, I finished my graduate degree and began working as a demonstration teacher in the University's School for Research on Language Disorders. Months later, your grandfather, *Papi*, pronounced with the Spanish or Portuguese *ah* sound, invited me to visit him in New York City where he was studying for his doctorate at Columbia University. While there, he asked me to marry him. I took advantage of that trip to apply for a special education teaching position in Westchester County, just north of New York City. I got the job for the following fall.

The summer of our engagement, I escorted a group of high school juniors and seniors to Peru with the Experiment in International Living. (Your dad participated in one of their summer programs to Mexico when he was in high school.) The students and I lived with families in Puno, on the shores of Lake Titicaca, at an altitude of 12,556 feet. Although it was our summer, we arrived in the dead of their winter. The winds whipped off the lake, and houses didn't have heat. The days, however, were sunny and cloudless. While there, I took the students by train to Machu Picchu, the most famous archaeological site in Peru. One day I hope we'll go there together. Meanwhile, Papi was doing research in Sâo Paulo, Brazil, so we had little contact except for an occasional letter that managed to survive the continental distance between us. My mother, in the meantime, became our wedding planner in Milwaukee.

We married at Our Savior Catholic Church on September 17, 1966. After the ceremony, a girl friend helped me move my things to New York City. I remember our confusion and apprehension upon entering the City after we emerged from the Lincoln Tunnel, under the Hudson River, into midtown Manhattan. We finally found International House, the Columbia student housing facility for students from all over the world. Your grandfather was a resident advisor there so we didn't have to pay rent for our tiny studio apartment.

Every work day I drove to and from Scarsdale on the Bronx River Expressway in my used pink and white Nash Rambler. Living in The Big Apple turned out to be an exciting place for this Milwaukee girl. Frequently, we'd receive free tickets to the opera, ballet, or other performances at Lincoln Center.

My wedding portrait, 1966, age twenty-seven

The following summer, Papi took an internship working with UNESCO in Paris. He flew over before me, and I joined him when the school year was over. It was in Paris that I told him I was pregnant. We lived in a charming old apartment on the Rue de Bac, not far from the Louvre. We had no refrigerator, so I had to shop every day, a good way to practice French.

With Papi during a visit to his home in Atlanta, 1967

## *Recife, Brazil and the Happiest Day of My Life*

**AFTER A BRIEF VISIT WITH FAMILY IN MILWAUKEE, WE HEADED FOR RECIFE, BRAZIL.** My Spanish served as a good foundation for the Portuguese language, although the latter was far more difficult to pronounce, and much of the vocabulary was different. We lived in a modest apartment on Avenida Bôa Viagem, across from the Atlantic Ocean. I could stick my head out of the side window from our apartment and see the water. (Later I also hung your dad's diapers on a line strung outside the window so they could dry in the sun.)

I spent my days studying Portuguese, reading, writing family and friends, visiting the market for our food, cooking, and preparing for my baby's delivery. There was no ultrasound yet, so we didn't know if the baby would be a boy or a girl, although it was common for Brazilian women to want to feel, rub, and listen to my belly, to tell me if the baby would be a boy or a girl. I really missed my parents then and knew how much my mother would have wanted to help me before and after the birth.

Women wore special maternity clothes then. The idea was to conceal your growing stomach. I had to visit a dressmaker to have maternity dresses made, although I had brought a few items from the U.S. I didn't have a proper bathing suit, so I had one made. It was rare for pregnant Brazilian women to go to the beach, and, if they did, they weren't seen in swimming suits. When I was about eight months pregnant, I crossed the street to the beach and went for a swim inside the reef for which Recife is named. I got tangled up in a school of Portuguese men-of-war. The pain on my arms was searing. Fortunately, the water was not over my head. I stood up, unable to pull the creatures off. A nearby fisherman came to my rescue by removing them, helping me out of the water, and rubbing sand over my arms to scrape off any toxic residue. I returned to the apartment to rest. Aside from the terrible welts I developed, I was lucky, and so was your father, for it could have been much more serious.

Your dad was born on March 18, 1968, at a small, private, maternity hospital named *Nossa Senhora de Fátima,* "Our Lady of Fatima." Fortunately, the clinic accepted our student health insurance. The public hospitals had few resources and often two women had to share one bed. Your dad was a big baby and quite pink compared to the Brazilian children born in the clinic that day.

Maternal instinct took over. Mom wasn't there to advise me, but I did have my books. And, although we were poor by U.S. standards, we could afford a housekeeper. Cecí came from the interior of northeastern Brazil, referred to as the sertâo, an arid place, where little grows. She had copper skin, curly hair, green eyes, and freckles—a beautiful blend of three races. When your dad was old enough for solid food, some of my State Department women friends, who had U.S. commissary privileges, would occasionally bring me jars of baby food, but I made most of it myself.

Nearby, on the same street, stood the mansions of the rich. We, on the other hand, were living on Papi's small research grant, but we were generally content with our place, despite its cramped, dark kitchen. Your dad slept in a screened crib to keep the mosquitoes from biting him, there being no screens on our windows. In the morning I'd occasionally find that he had scooted up so far in the crib that his head lay against the screen, covered in bites. I felt awful, wondering if he'd get some tropical disease. We could have closed the windows, but it would have been torturously hot.

We met two generous and down-to-earth Brazilian women friends who happened to live in our apartment building and worked in the same office as Papi. Silvia and Dadinha stood in for your dad's godparents at his baptism in a nearby Catholic church run by Maryknoll missionary priests. Those kind priests, knowing how economically stretched we were, donated some furniture to us.

# WATER SKIING ON THE AMAZON

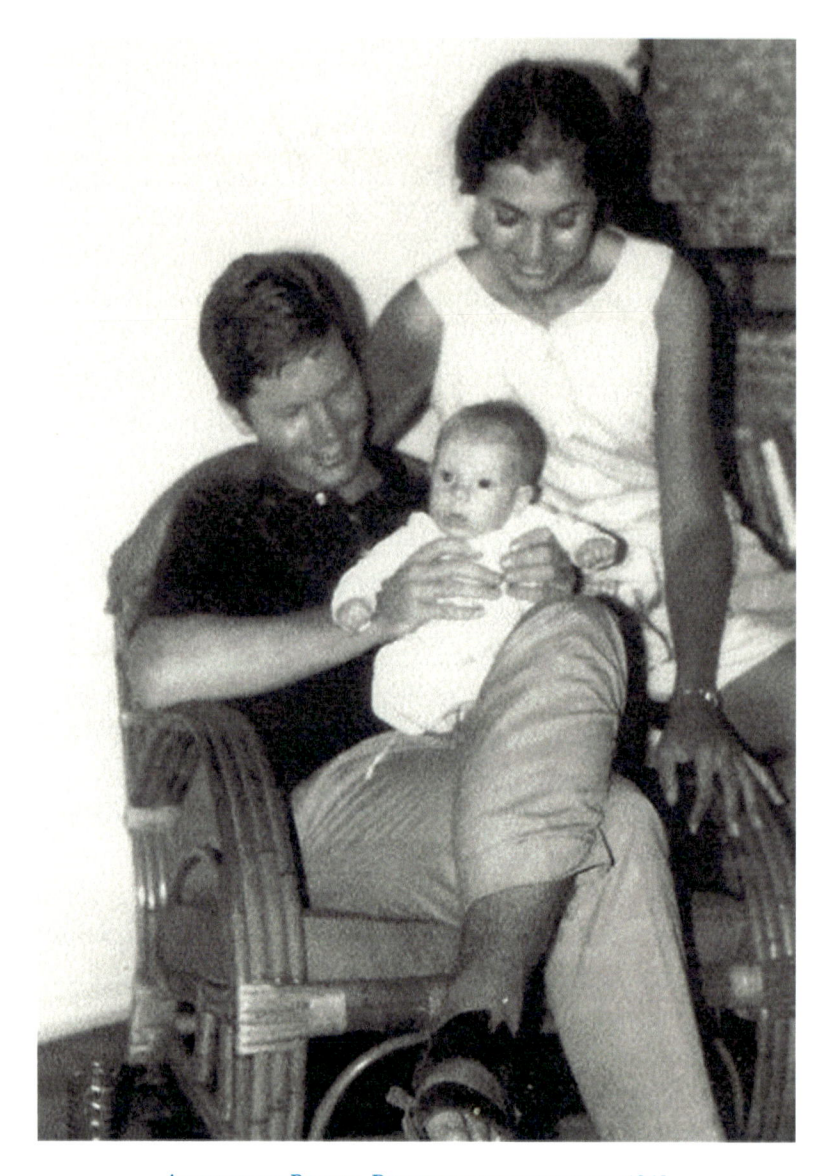

AT HOME IN RECIFE, BRAZIL WITH YOUR DAD, 1968

With Papi's research nearly completed, he applied for a job with the U.S. Agency for International Development. We returned to Milwaukee, where we lived with my parents who were eager to meet their first grandson. The employment offer finally came for Papi. We would live in Washington D.C for several weeks while he received orientation for his new assignment in Rio de Janeiro. There were vaccinations for all of us, and your dad, only nine months old, had to have his picture taken for his own diplomatic passport.

FOUR GENERATIONS IN MILWAUKEE: YOUR DAD WITH PAPI, YOUR GREAT-GRANDFATHER, JOHN SILKE, AND YOUR GREAT-GREAT-GRANDFATHER, HENRY SEITZ, BEFORE OUR MOVE TO BRAZIL, 1968

New York City, Paris, Recife, and now Rio de Janeiro! We took an eighth-floor apartment overlooking Copacabana Beach. It had a long balcony with glorious views of the Atlantic from our living, dining, and master bedroom. It was a dream apartment. At their suggestion, we hired Rita, the previous tenants' live-in housekeeper, who quickly warmed up to our resident baby boy. After a period of adjustment, I took advantage of Rita's conscientious care to do substitute teaching at the American School in Rio.

## *Divorce: Finding a New Life with My Son, Family, and Work*

**YOUR DAD LEARNED TO WALK IN RIO AT ABOUT THE SAME TIME THE RELATIONSHIP BETWEEN PAPI AND ME WAS TAKING A NEGATIVE TURN.** I had hoped we could work things out because, having been raised Catholic, I was taught that marriage was for life. But since then I've learned that, while a life-long marriage is the ideal, especially for the sake of the children, there may be complex circumstances that can't be changed or mended so that divorce becomes the only recourse. Whatever the circumstances, however, it is heart-breaking.

I left Rio in May, 1969 with your dad on my hip. Once again, we returned to my parents in Milwaukee until I could get on my feet. We eventually moved into an apartment above a butcher shop not too far from the university where I returned to teach in the School for Research and Language Disorders. Later we could afford an attractive two-bedroom apartment, and my parents and relatives helped to furnish it with decent, used furniture. Mom would take two busses and walk several blocks to get to our place to care for your dad until I found a woman who took babies and small children into her home.

It was tough getting used to Milwaukee's harsh winters again. We had no garage, so some mornings I'd have to leave your dad bundled up in his playpen while I ran outside to start the car engine and scrape the snow and ice from the windshield. Then I'd run back inside to get your father.

PATRICIA S. TAYLOR EDMISTEN

Your father, age two, with his grandmother, Dorothy Silke, 1970

## *Cocoa Beach and the Space Capital of the United States*

**IN 1971, LONGING TO RETURN TO A TROPICAL CLIMATE, YOUR DAD AND I MOVED TO COCOA BEACH.** The mermaid dream never came true, but we were in Florida. Equipped with my Master's degree, I took a job as coordinator of the specific learning disabilities program in Brevard County, Florida. Your three-year-old father stayed with my parents for a few weeks while I drove to Cocoa Beach in my royal blue Volkswagen with daisies on the doors that I had cut out of Contact paper. I had to keep a back windows open to accommodate a Schefflera plant. I scouted the beach area first and found a pretty townhouse at La Riviere, a small complex, with a glistening pool in the center, framed by tropical flowering plants. Perfect, I thought, if we could afford the $175.00 monthly rent. But it was only a block from the beach and had a second floor balcony off the master bedroom, overlooking the pool. I couldn't resist. Our first piece of furniture was a bright orange, imitation leather sofa that the managers gave us. Two weeks later, the moving van came with our things from Milwaukee, and my mother and your father arrived by plane.

It was the end of summer, and I had to find a good child care program for your dad while I worked. I enrolled your dad in a pre-school with a good reputation. It broke my heart to leave him the first day I started work. I could hear him wailing as I left him with his teacher and walked away. Weeks later his teacher told me that I needed to work with my son so that he learned to "color within the lines." She had no idea of my background in childhood development, but I gently explained that, at age three, children should be allowed to color freely, to experiment with shapes and colors until they developed the finer hand-eye coordination that is required before learning to color within the lines. She told me off. I withdrew your dad and found another pre-school affiliated with a Presbyterian church.

Your dad thrived at the church school. There's a little story I'll tell that touched me deeply. The children had been practicing for a Christmas performance. Your dad had memorized a little poem. He came out on the stage, this tow-headed little boy with a bowl cut, in a red blazer and blue pants. He recited his poem without a hitch, went back to join the other children, and, when the curtain came back up again, he beckoned me to get him, tears falling from his cheeks. I heard a lot of sympathetic chuckles from the other parents.

Another incident occurred after tornadoes whipped across the county. Although the tornadoes had passed, it was still very windy. Your dad, having been cooped up inside, wanted to go out to play. It was early in the morning. While I was getting dressed, I heard the front door slam, followed by screams. I ran downstairs and found that the door had slammed shut on your father's hand, nearly severing the tip of one of his fingers. I called for a neighbor to help and ran for a clean wash cloth to keep the finger intact and to prevent more blood loss. A neighbor took us to the pediatrician while I held the cloth firmly over the injury. I'll never forget your dad's screams when the doctor soaked his finger in an antibiotic solution before bandaging it without stitching it first. The finger healed, but I think, if you look closely, you'll still see a scar.

YOUR FATHER, AGE FOUR, WITH BANDAGED HAND, COCOA BEACH, FL, 1972

The decision to leave Milwaukee was not easy. I hated leaving my parents again, but they would be retiring to Florida in a few years, and, after their first visit, they decided to retire in Cocoa Beach. I loved its name, the tropical foliage, avocados, mangos, and citrus. We walked the one block to the beach nearly every day. After Brazil, the Milwaukee winters seemed brutal. The move would be the fresh start I needed, and I hoped my boy would flourish there. Coincidentally, this was the time when rocket science was burgeoning. Now Brevard County uses the title, "Florida's Space Coast" to attract tourists to the Kennedy Space Center in the area known as Cape Canaveral, the Spanish name for the sugar cane that used to grow there. From the beach, your daddy and I watched the Saturn V launches, part of NASA's Apollo and Skylab programs.

When our rent increased, we moved to a less expensive, second floor apartment with a balcony large enough for your dad to play. I bought a white kitty for him, and he named her "Clancy." Sadly, despite our efforts to keep her safe, Clancy escaped down the back stairs into the road where she was hit by a car.

## Dr. Patty: The University of Florida

**AFTER TWO YEARS IN COCOA BEACH, I RECEIVED A DOCTORAL FELLOWSHIP IN SPECIAL EDUCATION ADMINISTRATION AT THE UNIVERSITY OF FLORIDA IN GAINESVILLE.** I hired a driver and small truck, and, once again, your dad and I were on the move. Now he's five-years-old. We took an apartment at University Garden Terrace, a large complex, primarily occupied by graduate students and their families. There was a pond behind our unit and lots of green space for your dad to play with his new friends. He quickly adjusted to kindergarten, and I got down to my studies. I often felt guilty having to say no to him when he wanted to play while I had to do my assignments. I still made time, however, to take an occasional weekend trip to Cedar Key on the Gulf Coast, where we smelled the briny air and ate seafood at a restaurant on stilts over the mud flats.

Another of our favorite excursions was to the Devil's Millhopper, an enormous sinkhole that had a rough path circling down to the bottom. It seemed that we were descending into some primeval tropical paradise where a dinosaur might emerge at any moment. Twelve streams flowed into the pond at the bottom. You could sink your fingers into the sand and find sharks' teeth. We also tubed down the cold, spring-fed Ichetucknee River, an experience Disney couldn't begin to replicate. I'm hoping that soon we will all get together in north-central Florida to explore this treasure, now part of the Florida State Park system.

# WATER SKIING ON THE AMAZON

Your father in armor, age six, Gainesville, FL, 1974

## *Dorothy: A Generous and Adventurous Heart*

**MY MOTHER DOROTHY, YOUR GREAT GRANDMOTHER, CAME TO LIVE WITH US WHILE WE WERE IN GAINESVILLE.** She and your great-grandfather John were having problems after having been married thirty-five years. A brief separation seemed in order. Despite their occasional quarrels, my parents had always seemed happy, but children don't always know what is in their parents' hearts when it comes to their relationship with each other, especially after the children leave home. Mom was very depressed when she was with us so I arranged for her to get counseling. After several weeks with us, she decided that, if her marriage to my father couldn't be saved, she'd move to wherever your dad and I were living at the time, rent an apartment near us, and get training as a practical nurse. She would first return to Milwaukee, hoping for a reconciliation with my father.

Mom returned home just before Mother's Day in 1974. The last time I saw her she was in the little Gainesville airport. She wore an attractive yellow pant suit, and her hair was a soft silver. She had lost a lot of weight as a result of her depression, but she looked beautiful. Long story short, my parents couldn't work out their differences, and my mother, having been under the influence of barbiturates to help her sleep, took too many of them and died at age fifty-nine. (I've now lived sixteen years longer than she.)

# WATER SKIING ON THE AMAZON

My mother (your great-grandmother), Dorothy Silke, before her death, 1974

My eyes water as I write this part of the story. Your great grandmother would have loved you so much. She adored Florida and its beaches. She loved taking long walks, looking for shells. It didn't bother her too much that your dad and I were moving to Florida because she and my father were planning to join us when Dad turned sixty-two. Three years after Mom's death, Dad died of a heart attack, one year before he would have retired.

There is a quote by Cesar Vallejo, a Peruvian poet, now deceased: *Hay golpes en la vida tan fuerte, yo no sé,* "There are such awful blows in life; I don't understand." My mother's death was that kind of blow for me. She was a good, generous woman. In her suicide note, she asked God to forgive her. Because of her own suffering, I'm sure Mom never fully considered the pain her death would cause my father, brother, and me. I've always felt guilty, thinking that, had I been in Milwaukee, I would have been able to get help for her. Since then, I've learned that, no matter how painful life can be, there is always a window of escape, especially if you pray for help and confide your pain to a trusted family member or friend. It's easy for our thinking to become distorted when we're depressed. We give ourselves the wrong messages, and our feelings follow that distorted thinking. That's why it's important to speak to someone you trust when you're feeling that low. A good friend recently reminded me of some good advice: When you're feeling dreadful about something or depressed, "tell God and one person."

During my last semester at the University of Florida, still mourning my mother's death, we moved to Daytona Beach, where I had an internship teaching classes in specific learning disabilities at Bethune-Cookman, a predominantly black college. Before finding an upper flat on the beach, we lived in a small, inexpensive motel room. I'd prepare my lessons in the bathroom so I wouldn't disturb your father while he slept.

## Deep South, Y'all: Mobile and the University of South Alabama

**AFTER EARNING MY DOCTORATE IN 1975, WE MOVED TO MOBILE, ALABAMA.** I had wanted to stay in Florida, but there was a freeze on university hires throughout the State. Instead, I took a position in the Special Education Department at the University of South Alabama. Your dad had been happy in Gainesville and didn't want to leave until I promised him a kitty, once we were settled in Mobile. I kept my word, and we adopted a sweet runt of a litter from the humane society. Later, I learned she would have been classified as a Russian Blue. Less than a year later, "Smoky" surprised us when we found her in an upstairs closet with her own litter of adorable kittens for which we found homes. (Smoky lived a long happy life and even spent two summers with us in North Carolina.)

Again, I thought it necessary to remove your dad from one school and place him in another. I'm sure you can recall times when your parents felt you were being wrongly judged by an insensitive teacher, and they spoke with that teacher or took another action on your behalf, even if it might have been embarrassing for you. Most teachers are good at what they do, but one bad one is enough to cause damage. I had wanted your dad to go to a Catholic grade school and so enrolled him at St. Ignatius, considered to be one of Mobile's best schools. Unfortunately, he had the misfortune of being placed with a misguided teacher, and he became very unhappy. It's not easy trying to get ready to teach an 8:00 a.m. class when your child cries, insisting he wants to stay home. I tried to be reasonable with his teacher but she told me that I didn't know what I was talking about, so I removed your dad and put him in the local public school where he thrived. Did I meddle? Absolutely, and I'm glad I did.

WITH YOUR FATHER, AGE EIGHT, ON THE DAY OF HIS FIRST COMMUNION, MOBILE, 1976 (NOTE THE "HALO" OVER HIS HEAD.)

It was in Mobile that I met my friend Lynn whose son was your dad's age. Neither Lynn nor I had much of what today is called a "disposable" income, but we were both adventurous, and the four of us had many good times together. Lynn was an excellent sailor who took us out on Mobile Bay. The boys would hold onto a line and swing out away from the boat before jumping into the bay. A few times we pretended we were staying at the old, ritzy Grand Hotel at Point Clear, at the tip of Mobile Bay's Eastern Shore. The hotel had an enormous pool where we would take our boys. We affected such an air of confidence that no one would dare challenge our presence. Lynn and I remain close friends thirty-eight years later.

## *The Cradle of Naval Aviation: Pensacola and the University of West Florida*

**IN 1977, WE RETURNED TO FLORIDA WHERE I ACCEPTED A TEACHING POSITION IN SPECIAL EDUCATION AT THE UNIVERSITY OF WEST FLORIDA IN PENSACOLA, WHERE YOUR DAD SPENT MOST OF HIS CHILDHOOD.** It was here that I bought our first house on La Nain Drive. I had never lived in a single-family house before. My dad had just died, and my brother and I each received $5,000. from a Veteran's life insurance policy. I paid off our bills and put down ten percent, or $3,400. on a pretty three-bedroom, two bath-house in a pleasant neighborhood, not far from the university and close to good schools. As soon as I had saved a little money, I added a screened-in porch and, later, a fireplace. Friends put in a fish pond in the back yard, but we didn't have an aeration system, so the goldfish died, but the frogs and tadpoles loved it.

I couldn't wait for the weather to get chilly in October so we could have our first fire. I would ride my bike to house construction sites in an adjacent neighborhood and fill its wicker basket with scrap plywood.

Your father entered fourth grade at Scenic Height's Elementary School. He had dedicated and talented teachers there. Mrs. Sophia Papador, a refined, elegant woman came from Greece as a small girl. She had a special affection for your dad and inspired him to be a serious student. She loved teaching her students about Greek mythology.

Your dad took the school bus every day, and our cat Smoky often walked behind him on his way to the bus stop. Once there was a bully at the bus stop who threatened your dad. I could tell you the story as I remember it, but your dad would probably say it never happened that way, so you ask him. In any event, it was the catalyst that led to his taking Taekwondo, a Korean martial art. I took him to class twice a week and waited behind a one-way mirror that permitted parents to see their children. When he tested for red belt, he was the only one in the middle of the gymnasium floor at a local high school. Your dad looked so small down there, but he executed all his moves with the discipline he had practiced and broke the boards with spot-on kicks. Eventually, he achieved black belt.

# WATER SKIING ON THE AMAZON

Your father, age twelve, at a Taekwondo lesson, Pensacola, 1980

In sixth grade, your dad had a marketing teacher that should have retired years earlier. (Marketing in sixth grade?) This teacher must have taught the same curriculum for her entire career. She gave her students an assignment that required them to cut sale ads out of the newspaper. The students had to make scrap books of what items were on sale which months—linens in January--for example. It was a silly assignment, and your dad was already overloaded with homework and feeling the pressure. I would not have intervened in your dad's schooling had I not been so aware of the negative influence bad teaching can have on a child's attitude toward later education and of the positive impact of excellent teaching. (Keep in mind that, for years, I had taught and supervised student teachers in Wisconsin, Alabama. and Florida.) So here I was again, complaining to the principal about the irrelevance of this assignment. The principal said he had received other complaints from parents, but, because the teacher would soon retire, he asked me to simply drop the issue. I did, but your dad and I formed a team and completed that dumb project. I remember the two of us sitting on the floor with scissors, going through the newspapers, looking for ads to paste in a scrapbook.

By the time he started middle school, your dad's interest turned to surfing. On weekends during the cold winter months, I would wait in the car with my eyes glued on him. I don't know how I would have rescued him if he were in trouble out there in that dark, rough surf.

Your father, age fourteen, with his first surfboard, Pensacola, 1982

# WATER SKIING ON THE AMAZON

Although our lives were hectic in Pensacola, they were also full and rewarding. We'd go to the beach with friends and sometimes go canoeing on one of the pristine rivers in our area. Your dad attended lots of birthday parties at the roller skating rink. I frequently had 8:00 a.m. classes to teach so, like both of you now, we had to hurry week-day mornings, and we looked forward to weekends. Along the way, I attended the Bill Bond League baseball games your dad played as well as flag football. Oh, and I also rooted for him and the hand-made car he made for the Derby Day race when he was a Cub Scout.

WITH YOUR DAD, AGE FOURTEEN, PENSACOLA BEACH, 1982 (I'M FORTY-THREE.)

I would have my nine-month salary distributed over twelve months so that there would be income during the summer. I also began a separate savings account for your father's college expenses and managed to save a little each month for an occasional vacation.

In addition to traveling throughout Florida, we made yearly visits to Wisconsin to visit our family. We also went to Wyoming when your dad was ten with our good Cuban-American friend, Blanquita. We stayed at the

White Grass Ranch, and he became a "junior wrangler," working with authentic cowboys.

When your dad was fifteen, we went to Europe where we rented a tiny red car in Madrid and drove all over Andalusia. I remember that the car was tiny because it shook as smoke-belching trucks passed us as we wound around narrow mountain roads. We became terribly sick on our first night in Toledo. It had to have been the *paella*. We still managed to see the home of El Greco, painter, sculptor and architect of the Spanish Renaissance. In Granada we visited the Alhambra, a magnificent palace and fortress constructed in the year 899. It was re-built in the 12$^{th}$ century and used by the last Moslem leaders in Spain. We enjoyed an exciting Flamenco performance in Seville, one of the most beautiful cities in Spain. Still heading south, we visited the *Mezquita-catedral de Córdoba*, the Cathedral-Mosque, considered one of the most exquisite architectural gems of the world, named a World Heritage Site. The mosque became a cathedral after the Spanish drove the Moors out of Spain. In Cádiz, considered the oldest still-standing city in Europe, located on Spain's southwest Atlantic coast, I was proud of the way your dad ate a seafood stew with all kinds of shells and pincers protruding from a rich red broth. We crossed the Strait of Gibraltar by ferry and spent the day in Ceuta, also a Spanish City but on the African continent, sharing a border with Morocco. In Málaga we visited the hotel pool where women bathed topless. It was too late to blindfold your dad. Fortunately, he was wearing sunglasses that allowed him to stare unnoticed. It was in Málaga that your dad saw his first bullfight.

After Spain, we took a second-class car to Genoa, where we had time for lunch before changing trains. We went to a nearby hotel and used their bathrooms to wash up. In the dining room, given our limited budget, I struggled in Italian while ordering one entrée to share, but the waiter brought two. I sheepishly explained that I had meant to order only one, and he gracefully removed the second. After Genoa, we boarded our train to Garmisch, Bavaria, where your dad met his German relatives for the first time.

When your dad entered Woodham High School, I became what is now known as a "soccer mom." Soon he made the Varsity team, and I was driving him to and from practice and games. After Granddaddy Joe and I married in

1984, he and I would attend the games together. I don't think your dad knows it but, on those cold nights, we would bring a thermos of decaffeinated coffee, spiked with whisky, to keep us warm.

It's only been in recent years that your dad has occasionally mentioned to me how hard it was growing up without a father. This knowledge shouldn't have surprised me, but I had wanted so badly to compensate for his not having a dad at home that it hurt me to realize that he had hid his pain while he was young. Although I tried my best to encourage him in his studies and in his active sports life, pitching balls for him, rooting for him at games, I could not fill both roles of mother and father. My dad, your great-grandfather John, filled that role for a while, but he was in Wisconsin, and we only saw him twice a year after we moved to Cocoa Beach. When your dad was small, while we were still living in Milwaukee, it was Grandpa who would roughhouse with him. When Grandpa visited us in Gainesville, after my mother's death, he taught your dad how to ride a two-wheeler and took him fishing at Cedar Key. Unfortunately, Grandpa died in 1977, when your father was only nine. (I've come to realize that Papi's recent move to your Florida city was a good thing. He is near to love and protect you when your parents are not available, and he and your father have the opportunity to enjoy each other's company and deepen their relationship.)

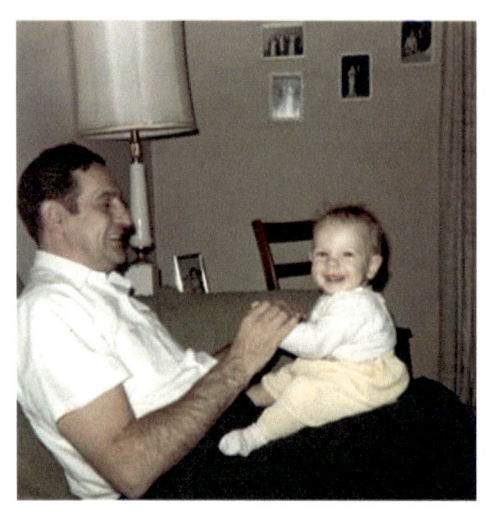

YOUR GREAT-GRANDPA, JOHN SILKE, WITH YOUR FATHER, SEVEN MONTHS, MILWAUKEE, 1968

PATRICIA S. TAYLOR EDMISTEN

## *Nicaragua #1: After the Revolution*

**IN 1981, I LEARNED ABOUT A FOOD POLICY STUDY TOUR TO NICARAGUA, SPONSORED BY OXFAM AMERICA, A FAMINE RELIEF ORGANIZATION THAT BEGAN IN EUROPE AFTER WORLD WAR II.** Nicaragua was at the tail end of a war with the "Contras." Thirty thousand people had been killed. For years, the United States had been on the wrong side of history by supporting the Somoza dictatorships through the training it provided their military officers on U.S. soil. Now we were financially backing the Contras, the leaders of the opposition to the new Sandinista government. At the time, I had been writing about the relationship between poverty and malnutrition in children and was curious about the situation in Nicaragua. I joined the Oxfam group of ten others who traveled around Nicaragua meeting with representatives of the Sandinista government, farmers, women rights advocates, teachers, and health workers.

At the time of our arrival, Nicaraguans were commemorating the anniversary of the death of publisher and writer, Pedro Joaquín Chamorro, who had apparently been assassinated upon the orders of the dictator, Anastasio Somoza Debayle. A devout Catholic, Chamorro had dedicated his publishing and writing life to achieving human rights for Nicaraguans, including the rights to assemble, vote, dissent, and the right to a free press. Chamorro had suffered torture and imprisonment because of his outspoken opposition to the Somoza regime.

While I was there, Chamorro's newspaper, *La Prensa*, now directed by his son, had re-issued the controversial essays his father had written. These pieces were strongly critical of the Somoza dictatorship. Reading his courageous words, I was convinced that people in the United States had to understand that it wasn't Communism that stoked the revolution. It was poverty, oppression, corruption, and the denial of human rights to the majority of Nicaraguans. I returned to the States and began translating Chamorro's political essays. I had hoped that a book of his essays would be snapped up by a U.S. publisher, but I was mistaken. Even presses that specialized in Latin American affairs wouldn't touch a book of translated essays. I finally decided to write a book about Chamorro, the man, and about the political division in his family that reflected the division in the nation. I would include some of his essays, and the work would be carefully documented, but I would take a journalistic approach, and there would be deep human interest.

## *Granddaddy Joe: "The World's Greatest Ecologist"*

**ABOUT TWO YEARS AFTER MY DIVORCE, I BEGAN TO THINK OF REMARRIAGE.** I started dating again in Cocoa Beach, but although I had met many attractive men, none demonstrated the maturity, integrity, and commitment I needed in a relationship. None, I thought, had what it took to be a loving stepfather. Most of them were connected with the space industry and loved the prestige they enjoyed by virtue of being affiliated with it. Then, in 1983, six years after moving to Pensacola, I met Joe Allen Edmisten at a Halloween party. Although I had earlier prayed that there would be a loving stepfather for your dad, by the time I was forty-four, I had stopped worrying about it. I was happy with my life, and your dad was already fifteen. He was who he was going to be, and I thought he was terrific in every dimension.

Dr. Joe Edmisten

FROM GRANDDADDY JOE'S WEBSITE, AGE SEVENTY-SIX, 2009

Granddaddy and I met at the home of a university colleague of mine who had also known Joe when he had been director of the Office of Environmental Education at the same university. Because it was Halloween, Joe was dressed in his academic regalia and had a *machete* hanging from his waist. Like the awful stereotype of a helpless woman, I couldn't open the wine bottle I had brought to the party, and Joe opened it for me. We started talking, and when I left to return home, he walked me to my car and said that "destiny" had brought us together, and that his heart "leaped" when he first saw me. Sigh. Well, I waited and waited for him to call, but he didn't.

The next time I saw Joe was at a League of Women Voter's fundraiser. It was a "roast and toast" of local politicians. We poked fun at the ones we thought were doing a lousy job and praised those who were excelling. On stage I played the part of Don Quixote de la Mancha, the elderly aristocrat who had read so many stories about chivalry that he imagined he was a knight who righted wrongs and protected maidens in distress. Quixote was the character in Miguel de Cervantes' *Man of La Mancha*, written between 1605 and 1615. Wearing a cardboard shield with fake sword in hand, I pretended to be a local county commissioner, known for "tilting at windmills," an expression referring to persons who undertake idealistic endeavors that have little chance of becoming reality. I also sang the lyrics from one of the songs from the musical, *Man of La Mancha*: "I am I, Don Quixote, the Lord of La Mancha, destroyer of evil am I…"

After I had changed into a cocktail dress, I felt that someone was staring at me. It seemed to be Joe, but he had lost so much weight I hardly recognized him. In fact, he looked a little like Don Quixote, without the armor and a lot more vulnerable. We struck up a conversation, and I mentioned that I was looking for property along the Blackwater River, a place that enchanted me. Joe told me he would look at the property to see if it was prone to flooding because that was part of what he did for a living. A few days later, we were on our way to the lot, and I learned he was going through a divorce, and that he had two little girls in addition to three older children from his first marriage. What was I getting into?

Joe advised me that the river-front lot had frequently flooded. That was the start of our courtship. Soon after, he brought a load of firewood to our house. He was an attentive boyfriend who was kind to Damian and generous to both of us. Two weeks before Christmas he went to south Florida for some consulting work. Before leaving, he gave me ten little white boxes that he had decorated with drawings of Christmas trees, candles, and ivy. I was to open a box each day while he was gone. Each box contained a different pair of tiny sterling silver earrings. Before his next trip, he left me a three-page letter that he had hand-written on a legal pad, telling me why he wanted to spend the rest of his life with me and asking me to marry him.

# WATER SKIING ON THE AMAZON

I was very nervous about being wife to a man who had been married twice before. Did he have some great flaw that would only come out after we were married? Of course, he might have asked the same thing of me. This was a joyful time for me, but I was also filled with apprehension. By then I had been a single parent for fifteen years.

There is a gorgeous nature trail at the University of West Florida that, coincidentally, your Granddaddy conceived and executed. During that period of indecision, every work day I would eat my lunch on a wood bench, overlooking the quiet pond at the start of the trail, enjoying the wading birds and the fish hiding in the grassy margins of the bayou. I prayed for God's guidance in making the right decision, not only for myself, but especially for my son.

Joe surprised your father by giving him a very long, older model, gas-guzzling station wagon for his sixteenth birthday, a car with a lot of steel to protect the driver. We called it the "brown bomber." How many boyfriends would do such a thing? I'm sure your dad had hoped for something more streamlined, but he kept those thoughts to himself and thanked Joe.

During my spring break Joe took me to meet his family on a large farm in Boone, NC. His family was enormous—four brothers, one sister, aunts, uncles, cousins everywhere. He pointed out which relatives lived in which *holler*, "hollow," the term people from Appalachia use to refer to a valley. I couldn't keep everyone straight. His mom and dad, *mamaw and papaw*, were happy, welcoming people. There was no artificiality in them. They said what came to mind and practiced their religion the way that Jesus intended. They gave generously of the bounty of their garden to all who were in need, and they spoke ill of no one. Joe announced our engagement to them. They probably wondered who was this Yankee (and Catholic) woman coming into their profoundly Baptist lives, but if they had doubts, they concealed them. Later, after our marriage, Papaw would tease me by calling me Priscilla or Phyllis before getting to Patricia.

GRANDDADDY'S PARENTS, WALTER AND NELLIE MAE EDMISTEN, BOONE, NC, 1994

Joe and I married on May 19, 1984 at the chapel of the First Presbyterian Church in downtown Pensacola. It was an intimate wedding with family and close friends. Your sixteen-year-old father was there, as were Uncle John and Aunt Lana who came from Milwaukee. Great Aunt Eleanor came from Chicago, and Great Aunt Lucy and Uncle Martin came from New York. Joe's daughter, Sarah, attended as did his youngest daughters, Brook, age three, and Rebecca, five. (As you know, Granddaddy also has a daughter, Sharon, who taught Earth Science and lives in Norfolk, VA and a son, Allen, a prison chaplain, who lives in South Carolina with his family.) Since that wedding I have gained five step-children, two biological grandchildren, and fourteen step-grandchildren. (On March 12, 2008, after Granddaddy Joe's first wife, Margaret, died, we had our marriage blessed during a Mass celebrated by Fr. Dennis O'Brien at St. Rose of Lima Catholic Church, Milton, Florida.)

# WATER SKIING ON THE AMAZON

At our reception: Granddaddy, age fifty-one, Grandmother, forty-five, Pensacola, 1984

# PATRICIA S. TAYLOR EDMISTEN

*At the wedding reception, with your father, age sixteen, Pensacola, 1984*

## Montezuma's Reward

**AS I WRITE THIS SECTION, I'M WONDERING HOW I'LL GET EVERYTHING TOGETHER IN TIME TO MIGRATE TO MONTEZUMA, NORTH CAROLINA FOR THE SUMMER.** This will be our thirtieth year, although before we were retired, we might drive back and forth a few times each summer to escape the heat in Pensacola. Each year, despite the hot temperatures in Pensacola, I'm apprehensive about leaving our comfortable home and making the six hundred-mile trip to our 1896 farmhouse in Montezuma. Once I'm there, however, after the sheets have been removed from the furniture, after the disposal of field mice droppings, the removal of spider webs, and after everything is reasonably clean, we settle into a satisfying routine. We smell the ripe fragrance of apples that have been stored in the spring house and the clean cool air, scented by fir trees, wild roses, and the "Sweet Bubba" bush that has flowers that smell like grape Kool-Aid. Not a late sleeper, I often sit on the side porch at dawn, where I see the fog rise and hear the swelling chorus of birds. In the evening, we enjoy our cocktail on the same porch. Before bed, we might stand under the black sky, watching the stars in their ever-expanding universe.

I love the reward of the fresh lettuce you both have picked for our salads and the tart taste of the sauce I make from the Transparent apples. You've picked the raspberries that are transformed into luscious jam. Some years we have an abundance of wild blackberries with juice that will become dark purple jelly with the sweet, complex taste of an expensive Port wine.

I cherish my walks alone, or with family and friends, along the many paths that Granddaddy keeps open on our land. I am blessed to have met owl, deer, fox, and wild turkey. The bear scat I have found keeps me alert and reminds me that, should I encounter one, I must make myself appear as big as possible, lift up my arms, wave my walking stick, and shout. I hope I can remember all of that should I meet a black bear face-to-face.

In June, the lightning bugs greet one another with SOS flashes. "Let's get together," they signal to one another, with loving luminescence.

When you're here I enjoy seeing your pleasure when you eat marshmallows toasted to perfection over the bonfire. My heart remembers that you sailed the little boats Granddaddy made for you in our stream, and that he taught you how to carve beautiful and useful walking sticks and how to walk on his home-made stilts. You also learned how to use a slingshot and hit your target. Then there was the surprise, on your first visit to Montezuma, when you were four, Sophie, and Vincent two, when you opened the swollen bud on the Jewelweed, sometimes known as Touch-me-not. To build up the tension, Granddaddy kept warning you to be careful, to squeeze the pod with caution. You were so apprehensive that, when you finally touched the end of the seed pot, and it exploded, sending seeds in every direction, you jumped back and laughed when you realized he had been kidding you. Vincent, you wanted to know the name of the round, spongy things we kept seeing on the Spring Path. After you knew the name, you exclaimed, "More mushrooms!" with each new sighting.

Over the years we've been visited by many friendly dogs who have adopted us each summer, starting with Minnie and Maxie, who always traveled together. Then came a host of others, including Ralph, our favorite mutt, who made our place his summer home for many years. Abbie, the black lab, and Maggie, the blonde lab that you love, Sophie, came next. Maggie still visits each day, hoping for a hand-out and a good petting.

My favorite time here is when the fog descends and envelopes the house and woods. You can barely make out the mountain behind the house. When I walk in the fog I feel as if I'm inside a cloud.

It gladdens me to know that our mountain place has a special place in your father's heart, and that you have also come to love it. Right now there is political turmoil and violence around the world, especially in the Middle East. I'm filled with empathy for the people who suffer, but I feel hope when I watch the birds at our feeder, see the bright yellow and orange flowers of the Jewelweed, observe the progress our corn has made, watch our apples mature and the chestnut trees flower. Here there is peace. Here is life as God intended it.

# WATER SKIING ON THE AMAZON

Montezuma's Reward, 2012

## Cuba #1: "The Enemy" Ninety Miles off our Shore

**IN 1986, I WENT TO CUBA FOR THE FIRST TIME.** Remember that my mother and her cousin visited Cuba in 1938, and I had long been curious about seeing this island-nation that has defied every attempt of the United States to bring it under control.

Between 1953 and 1957, a young, audacious Fidel Castro led a rebellion that became an island-wide revolution that toppled the dictator Batista. Castro became Head-of-State. Fifty-seven years later, he still lives, and the majority of Cubans still honor him because he improved their lives. He brought health care to them and eradicated illiteracy by training high school students to teach reading throughout the island. All children had access to higher education if they studied hard.

Before Castro, racism on the island was rampant, even though the majority of its inhabitants are of mixed race. A minority, however, felt themselves superior because they had inherited "pure" Spanish blood. These people tended to be the richest and most powerful. (They were also those who had the most to lose after the revolution.) Depending upon physical features, under no one's control, many Cubans had been denied access to adequate housing, food, education, beaches, restaurants, and clubs until Castro countered this deep racism through legislation. He also, for example, pointed to his own springy hair and said, "In Cuba we are all a little bit black."

Although Castro did much to restore the dignity of the poor, it can't be denied that the wealthy also suffered. As that wise saying goes, "more than one thing can be true." Thousands of Cubans left their land and homes for Miami. Their elegant houses were confiscated by the government and are still used for offices or *casas de protocol*, "protocol houses," to host visiting guests. It was in one of those houses near the sea that I stayed during my first visit. In many cases, families were split up because the elderly didn't want to leave their homes and may not have been healthy enough to endure displacement.

During that first visit, I traveled with a small group of university professors from around the country, under the sponsorship of the Cuban Studies Association in New York. We visited an array of schools, from pre-school through university. Should you be interested one day, you can read my *Cuban Journal* to get all the details. It was hard to break away from the official "minder" who accompanied us to ensure that the impressions we got of Cuba were the ones the government wanted us to take back with us, but I managed to break away a few times. I took a public bus to a Catholic seminary where I met with the director. The seminary was empty at the time because, although a few churches were open, religious education and practice had been discouraged by the revolutionary government. Some parents had their children secretly baptized to avoid being accused of counter-revolutionary behavior.

On my first Sunday, I attended Mass in the Havana Cathedral, begun by the Spanish in 1748. Mass was surprisingly well attended, with many men standing in the back. A week later, however, on Easter, I wanted to attend a different church and had to ask many people before I learned where I could find an open one. In my quest, I boarded a *camelo*, a public bus called a "camel" because it had two "humps," two connected cars. I succeeded in attending Mass in a small neighborhood church where people joyfully wished me *Felices Pascuas* (Happy Easter).

Each vicinity in Havana has its own "neighborhood watch" program where "comrades" are chosen to oversee the comings and goings of the people who live in their area. They report any behavior that seems out-of-line with current revolutionary thought.

During the early evenings, I would break away from my group and walk down to the Malecón, the breakwater and sidewalk that run along the Caribbean Sea. Young couples strolled hand-in-hand. I would sit on the sea wall and be surrounded by young adults who asked me about life in the United States. Most expressed the desire to visit. They told me that, although they had good educations, they had little freedom in choosing their careers. It is the State that determines, depending upon its needs, what a student seeking higher education will study. Imagine having to study what the government chooses for you. How much initiative and motivation would you have?

The students who don't pass required State examinations study in vocational colleges where they receive training that helps provide the country with a skilled labor force. Students graduate without debt because the government pays for all education. Even in pre-school students learn that manual labor has its own dignity, that someone who does manual labor should be respected. A feature of the Cuban economic system that most mystifies and upsets U.S. citizens is that a garbage man and a medical doctor might receive nearly the same salary.

On another of my break-away ventures, I arranged to secretly meet a professor from the University of Havana who had been our guide during the group visit to the University. We met at a crowded restaurant. He brought a student so our meeting wouldn't look suspicious. He was a Catholic and told me how hard it was to practice his religion because those who did were denied promotions and made to look foolish. I learned that the freedom of expression we take for granted is still denied in Cuba.

While visiting a neighborhood medical clinic, I asked an elderly lady about the service she received there. She told me that she felt fortunate to be seen by a doctor but that the clinic could not provide the medicines she most needed.

The United States still doesn't trade with Cuba, although now, at least, certain medicines and supplies are allowed into the country. There is an interesting contradiction in our policies: Recently, when I went to buy fish for dinner, I asked about the origins of the fish on display. The farm-raised Tilapia came from China, still a staunchly Communist country that continues to suppress its people, and the grouper-like, farm-raised Basa came from Viet Nam, also a Communist country. Both China and Viet Nam enjoy brisk trade with the U.S. I don't think that keeping Cuba closed off from the United States, while the rest of the world trades with them, will bring democracy to Cuba. It does, however, communicate that we are still their enemy.

Had I only traveled with my group and our Cuban "minder," I would not have gained such a rich appreciation of the people and their hardships. It's also significant that I could not have had any of those experiences had I not been able to speak Spanish. Once back in the U.S., I wrote articles on my experiences there, did slide presentations, and introduced many to the human side of Cuba. As a result of my trip to Nicaragua in 1981, and my 1986 trip to Cuba, our Pensacola phone was tapped. We heard the recording device "tapping" in the background. Also, a few years later, I requested my file from the CIA. It arrived with most of the information blacked out, so that no sense could be made of it.

*Havana, Cuba, Cathedral in background, 1986*

## Nicaragua #2: Smuggling Censored Newspapers to the Future President

AS I NOTED EARLIER, WHEN I RETURNED FROM MY FIRST TRIP TO NICARAGUA IN 1981, I BEGAN TO TRANSLATE THE ESSAYS OF PEDRO JOAQUÍN CHAMORRO, THE PUBLISHER AND EDITOR OF *LA PRENSA* ("THE PRESS"), THE MAJOR NICARAGUAN NEWSPAPER. I was certain that, if U.S. citizens learned that the Nicaraguan revolution was more the result of rampant inequality and deprivation than the result of Communist infiltration, we would stop arming the Contras, the anti-revolutionary forces fighting the Sandinistas. I also mentioned that I had decided to write a nonfiction book about Pedro Joaquín Chamorro and his family but that would mean I'd have to return to Nicaragua to do the research.

Toward that end, I made calls to Chamorro's son, also named Pedro Joaquín, who was living in exile in San José, Costa Rica. He arranged for me to meet his mother, Doña Violeta Barrios de Chamorro, who, in 1990, would become the first woman president of Nicaragua, the first woman president of the Americas, and the second in the western hemisphere. (People forget that citizens of Canada, Mexico, Central America, and South America are also Americans. In fact, along with our Native Americans, their indigenous peoples were the original Americans.)

I requested leave-of-absence from the University, and, in the summer of 1985, using my own money, and leaving my teen-age son with Granddaddy, I set off alone for Nicaragua. The young Pedro Joaquín met me at the San José, Costa Rica airport before I took my flight to Managua, the capital. He asked that I hide within my personal belongings issues of *La Prensa*, the family newspaper that was being published in Costa Rica because the Sandinistas were now doing the censoring. I agreed but was nervous about smuggling those papers because I knew the Sandinistas wouldn't tolerate the importation of anything that might undermined their achievements, and I was afraid of going to jail.

I tried to look casual as I went through customs, telling the fierce-looking guard that I was in Nicaragua to write a book about the revolution. Having made it through customs, I realized that my solo adventure was just beginning. I no longer could rely on a group leader to smooth the path for me like I had during my first visit in 1981.

Little had been done to rebuild Managua after the devastating earthquake that ripped it apart in 1972 when Anastasio Somoza Debayle was still in control. Six thousand died; twenty thousand injured, and 250 thousand were left homeless. The Cathedral was still a shell. The Inter-American Hotel, where I stayed, was one of the few remaining buildings higher than one story. It was filled with men who looked like foreign mercenaries (paid civilian soldiers). They resembled guys auditioning for a violent action movie, only this was real life.

Because of the earthquake destruction, there were no street signs. People in Managua no longer used street addresses when they told people where they lived. You would go to where the *arbolito,* "the little tree," used to be, or turn left "where the meat market was," phrases not helpful to an outsider. Instead of instructing someone to go north, they would say, go toward the *montaña,* the "mountain," Or, if the destination was south, they would say, walk toward *el lago,* "the lake."

It would have been too expensive for me to pay for all my expenses in dollars because the official exchange rate for the Nicaraguan currency, the *córdoba,* was so steep. This situation forced me to take advantage of the black market. Another researcher gave me detailed directions so that I could find a man who ran an illegal currency exchange. I set off by foot from the hotel, using his hand-drawn map, frequently looking over my shoulder to see if I was being followed. The currency exchange man lived in a tiny house on a dirt road, and he was eager to do business. Everyone wanted dollars then, so he offered me a much better exchange than I could have secured elsewhere. I broke the law and didn't feel good about it.

Managua in summer is a sweltering place. Even though it should have been the rainy season, it was very dry. There was almost no public transportation. The vehicles were decrepit, and there was no money for repairs. People got around in dilapidated cars owned by individuals who ran them like collective taxis. You had to stand on a corner a long time, signaling with your arm that you needed a ride, hoping that someone would stop. A driver would stop if he thought he could squeeze in one more person, and that meant that a stranger might sit on your lap, or you'd sit on theirs. One day I was so thirsty I thought I'd pass out. The car that stopped for me had part of the floor missing, so I could see the street below.

While in Managua, I met with all but one of Chamorro's four children. I had already met the younger Pedro Joaquín who was publishing anti-Sandinista essays. His sister, Christina, was also opposed to the revolutionaries, while their sister, Claudia, was working with them. Chamorro's other son, Carlos, who I did not see, was director of the pro-Sandinista newspaper, *Barricada* (Barricade). So two of Chamorro's children supported the Contras, and two were on the side of the Sandinistas. I also met with the elder Chamorro's brother, Jaime, who supported the Sandinistas and with his sister, Ligia, who opposed them. The family was split right down the middle. You'd think that kind of political division would have created grave tension in the family, but every one of the children believed they were carrying out their father's legacy, his quest for social justice, and they respected one another. Despite, the political division in the family after their father's death, all the children joined with their mother, Violeta, for Sunday dinner, where they remained family, joined by blood and loyalty to their parents.

One of the most memorable interviews took place when I met Chamorro's widow, Doña Viloleta. She warmly greeted me at her gracious home in Las Palmas, a pretty tree-shaded neighborhood. She showed me the glass-enclosed shrine she had created in honor of her husband. Inside the case was the bloody shirt he wore when he was assassinated after having made a visit to the Catholic Church, where he said his prayers each morning before work. He had been gunned down at an intersection by men wielding machine guns. His 1978 assassination is thought to have been the catalyst that started the revolution.

You've probably heard the expression, "The pen is mightier than the sword," attributed to Edward Bulwer-Lytton. In this instance Chamorro had fought Somoza with his typewriter (the pen), and Somoza fought him with prison, torture, and ultimately, death (the sword). But Pedro Joaquín's words won over the sword. It is he who is the hero; he who is remembered; he who inspires. One of the hallmarks of democracy is freedom of the press.

Citizens must be exposed to competing ideas in order for them to make informed decisions about their governments.

Doña Violeta offered me a rum and coke, and we sat in rocking chairs in the family's cool den. Later we shared a meal of *Moros y Cristianos* ("Moors and Christians," dark red beans and rice). That afternoon, knowing I had been trained in special education, Doña Violeta took me to a school for handicapped children that was run by a friend of hers, a school I later supported.

The following day I accompanied Doña Violeta to the offices of *La Prensa* where I met with several journalists who were close friends of Chamorro. I recorded those interviews so that, when I returned to the States, I could accurately transcribe them from Spanish to English. Quotes from those interviews appear in my book, *Nicaragua Divided: La Prensa and the Chamorro Legacy*, that I hope you'll read in the future.

After the heat, the difficulty getting around, and missing my family, I was eager to return to Pensacola. Now I needed to safely smuggle out from Nicaragua the many documents and books the Chamorro family had given me as well as the tapes from the interviews. At the airport, some young guard, impressed with his own power, dumped out all of my belongings on a table. He made a quick visual inventory, messing everything up, but didn't confiscate anything. I would have loved to have told him off but didn't dare. I quietly re-packed everything and got on that plane.

## *Religion and Patriotism: a Dangerous Mix*

**IN 1986, I HEARD ON NATIONAL PUBLIC RADIO THAT NICARAGUAN "CONTRAS," THE MEN WHO WERE FIGHTING AGAINST THE SANDINISTAS, WERE RECEIVING MILITARY TRAINING AT HURLBURT AIR FORCE BASE, JUST EAST OF PENSACOLA.** I told Granddaddy that I had to publicly dissent. He agreed to join me in a protest outside the gates of the Air Force Base. I called a few other like-minded friends. Three Maryknoll priests, who had been visiting Pensacola, joined us, men who had worked for years among the poor in Latin America. A small group of us stood outside the gates of the military installation holding protest signs that first Saturday morning. After an hour, two of the priests crossed over the yellow line at the check point of the Base. They were immediately arrested. Our group grew each Saturday until we numbered two hundred and fifty. It was at that demonstration that the faculty and students of Liberty Bible College in Pensacola, thinking our protests were sponsored by the Catholic Church (the arrest of priests), came out in force. They stood on the median separating the traffic on busy Highway 98, carrying signs that read, "Roman Catholic Bishops will Burn in Hell," "Nuke the Vatican," and "Jesus is not a Wafer." They taunted us to pray the rosary while we stood silently with our arms linked. There's a reason for separation of Church and State. When mixed, they can incite much hatred and even violence, as we see when men and women commit mass murder in the name of God. That to me is the real blasphemy.

## Nicaragua #3: Attending the Inauguration of the First Woman President in the Americas

**IN 1990, JUST AFTER THE PUBLICATION OF MY BOOK, I ATTENDED THE INAUGURATION OF MRS.** Chamorro, who became president in a democratically conducted election. She ran as the nominee for the United Nicaraguan Opposition, a coalition of political parties opposing the Sandinistas who, by then, were betraying some of their own ideals of making Nicaragua a just society. Few people in the United States knew anything about Mrs. Chamorro or her family, so my book was released at a favorable time. Bob Edwards, a nationally-known journalist and broadcaster, interviewed me on National Public Radio regarding the first woman president in the Americas.

VIOLETA BARRIOS DE CHAMORRO, PRESIDENT OF NICARAGUA, AT HER INAUGURAL CELEBRATION, 1990

(my photo)

# The United Nations: The Special Burdens of Poor Women

IN 1992, WHILE I WAS DIRECTOR OF INTERNATIONAL EDUCATION AND PROGRAMS AT THE UNIVERSITY OF WEST FLORIDA, I WAS INVITED TO SERVE AS A CONSULTANT FOR UNIFEM, THE ENTITY OF THE UNITED NATIONS THAT FUNDS PROGRAMS EFFECTIVE IN MEETING THE NEEDS OF WOMEN IN POOR COUNTRIES. I traveled to Sâo Paulo and Rio de Janeiro, Brazil to work with *Red Mulher* (the Women's Network), where I met with leaders who took me to observe their health and education projects.

In Peru, I worked with women from the *Flora Tristán Centro de la Mujer Peruana* (Flora Tristán Center of the Peruvian Woman). I visited health clinics that conducted cancer screenings and other medical services, along with civic education for poor women. At these centers the women learned about their rights, including the right to vote and the right to be free from domestic violence. I visited communal kitchens where mothers pooled their food in one large kitchen and took turns cooking to provide one nutritious meal daily for all their neighbors. I saw the happy looks of children in these same *pueblos jóvenes* (young towns) when they received their daily cup of milk in the *Vaso de Leche* program. When I returned to the U.S., I wrote comprehensive reports on all the programs I visited so that United Nations funding would be continued.

It was in Nicaragua that I learned about Pedro Joaquín Chamorro and his life-long struggle against the Somoza family of dictators. In Peru I learned about María Elena Moyano who had been assassinated by *Sendero Luminoso*, the Shining Path, a terrorist organization that would eliminate anyone who got in the way of their efforts to topple the Peruvian government. They used torture and death to achieve their ends, especially among the indigenous people who had no power to fight back. The members of *Sendero* also tried to organize people in poor neighborhoods surrounding Lima, Peru's capital. Their leaders called for a general strike and wanted everyone to refuse to work as a means to protest the government.

María Elena was in her early thirties. She had been raised in *Villa El Salvador*, a poor community of over 300,000 people, near Lima. Familiar with her leadership skills, the people of Villa El Salvador elected her to be their deputy mayor. She had been active in a network of women's organizations that work to improve living conditions. María Elena refused to ask her people to strike because she believed they needed to work to support their families. She knew that the government was corrupt, and that the National Guard, military, and police were brutal in their suppression of dissent. She stood up to all of them. She spoke "truth to power," an especially dangerous activity for a Latin American woman. *Sendero* would not abide this woman's disobedience, and so they assassinated her in front of her two young children at a community gathering. After her death, she became a powerful symbol for women all over Latin America who struggle for equal rights.

I asked permission to translate the autobiography María Elena had been writing before her death with the help of Diana Miloslavic Tupac, a friend and scholar from the Flora Tristán Center. Permission granted, I undertook the translation, introduction, and afterword to the book that was later published by The University of Florida Press. I contributed the royalties to support the work of the Center. I hope one day you'll read, *The Autobiography of María Elena Moyano: The Life and Death of a Peruvian Activist*.

## Cuba #2: Befriending "The Enemy" through Student and Faculty Exchanges

ONE OF MY FIRST EFFORTS AFTER BECOMING DIRECTOR OF INTERNATIONAL EDUCATION AND PROGRAMS WAS TO ARRANGE FOR AN EXCHANGE PROGRAM BETWEEN THE UNIVERSITY OF WEST FLORIDA AND THE UNIVERSITY OF HAVANA. It took a long time to get a visa from the Cuban government, and there were hoops I had to jump through to be approved for travel to Cuba by our State Department. This was still the time when few U.S. citizens could travel to Cuba, and those who did were suspected of undermining our foreign policy by spending money in Cuba. Even now, if you're not a Cuban-American, or not affiliated with an educational or cultural group that has a license, and you want to visit Cuba on your own, you have to enter from another country, like Canada or Mexico, and you have to ask the Cubans not to stamp your passport when you enter and leave.

With my documents in hand, I waited to board my flight to Havana. One of the most unusual spectacles occurred in the waiting area. Cubans returning to their country publicly accommodated on their bodies every purchase they had made in Miami. Women wore enormous skirts with petticoats lined with pockets. They tucked even heavy items in these pockets and looked as if each had gained fifty pounds. Men wore all their new clothes, one shirt on top of another. I don't know who they were trying to kid, but there must have been some rule forbidding the importation of anything a Cuban might re-sell for profit. Obviously, those who worked in customs turned a blind eye to this wide-spread behavior.

The flight lasted about thirty minutes. Long story short, I succeeded in signing an exchange agreement with the University of Havana, one of only eight such programs in the United States. While there I met two women professors who invited me to their homes and talked about the hardships with which the average Cuban family lives, especially the shortage of basic foods and household items. The women took me to visit a poor farming family who lived in the interior on the way to a beautiful mountain resort in Pinar del Rio. The contrast between their humble dwelling and the resort, visited by rich foreign tourists, was striking.

The women also took me to one of Havana's national "stores" where Cubans go to get basic supplies like beans, rice, cooking oil, and soap. Rough, gray boards were used as shelves, and there was no variety in the categories of goods available. Shopping in a State store is not like entering a Florida Publix where you must choose from over fifty kinds of cereal, for example. Citizens used ration cards to get a weekly share of rice, beans, and oil to last one week. Milk and eggs were hard to find. If shoppers were lucky, they might find chicken necks for protein. All the best foods were saved for visitors who stayed in the tourist hotels, like the elegant Hotel Nacional, where my mother and her cousin stayed in 1938, and where I stayed in 1986. I still shake my head at the ludicrousness of this situation in a country so close to the United States.

Although Castro did a lot to improve the lives of the poorest Cubans, the communist ideal has never been realized in any country. Instead of sharing equally in the benefits of society, hard working farmers are forced to sell their produce to the State. Maybe a tiny portion can be held back for their families, but it's never enough to sustain them. When you remove the satisfaction that comes from hard work by forcing workers to give away the fruits of their labor, you remove the incentive to work, so even the State has less and less to share with its citizens. That situation is slowly changing in Cuba, and farmers are now allowed to sell excess produce to support their families.

"Dollar" stores are curious contradictions. These stores are loaded with extravagant consumer goods, like electronics, perfumes, designer clothing, gourmet foods, chocolate, etc. The catch is that you must have American dollars to buy anything. The dollars help the State trade with other countries, but the average Cuban can't access those goods because they don't have access to dollars. Only people who are in certain tourism-related jobs have access, like taxi drivers and tour guides.

My biggest obstacle never occurred in Cuba, however. It took place in a conference room at my university after my return. Two Cuban-American professors demanded that I justify my actions before a committee. When they were children, their families had taken them to the States after Castro came to power. Understandably, having lost their homes and properties, their way of life, these families remained ardently opposed to any policy that might help Cuba.

Before my trip, I had sought permission from the University's president, so my opponents had no case, but they still created problems for me. My argument was then, and still is, that democracy is not spread or cultivated through policies that exclude and weaken a people. It is spread through contact and education. Those professors remained opposed to the exchange program, but it moved forward, and the professors and students who came to our university contributed to our understanding of Cuba and its people. Likewise, the professors from my university who taught in Cuba brought back a wealth of knowledge to share with their students. Unfortunately, once I retired and left the university, my successor suspended the program.

## Semester at Sea: Circumnavigating the Earth in One Semester

**IN 1997, GRANDDADDY JOE AND I APPLIED FOR TEACHING POSITIONS WITH THE SEMESTER AT SEA PROGRAM, THEN SPONSORED BY THE UNIVERSITY OF PITTSBURGH.** If accepted, we would circumnavigate the globe and be at sea for fourteen weeks, one hundred seven days, a full semester. We had to gear our course proposals to the countries we'd be visiting. We never thought that both of us would be accepted and had decided that, if one of us were accepted, the other would go as a "spouse" for $3,000., a remarkably low price given the length of the voyage. We were both accepted! Granddaddy would teach two ecology classes, one for beginners and one for more advanced students. I would teach three classes: Wealth, Power, and Democracy; Humanity and Global Resources; and Women's Issues in Developing Countries.

In addition to packing for three and one-half months, for all kinds of weather, we had to close down our historic house in Pensacola. (It was built in 1882, just twenty-one years after the start of the Civil War.) Your dad helped us by paying our bills and looking after the house. Fortunately for us, he had returned to Pensacola by then after earning his law degree and practicing in Miami for a while. He and your mother married in Pensacola, and while we were aboard the ship on the other side of the world, we received a fax of the ultrasound announcing the future birth of Sophie, my first grandchild. Vincent, you followed almost two years later, so even though you both left Pensacola in 2001, shortly after 9/11, you have ties to Pensacola, where you were both born and baptized.

In early February, 1998, we gathered with twenty-eight other faculty members for orientation on the S.S. Universe Explorer, docked in Nassau, the Bahamas. We had a tiny cabin on the Sun Deck. We never expected luxury, but we thought our cabin should have been larger, given the length of the voyage and the fact that both of us would have to cram all our personal items and teaching materials into that dinky space. There was a full bed, a tiny closet, a few drawers, and a bathroom with a shower so small you couldn't bend down to pick up a piece of soap. Oh, and there was a small porthole through which we could see the calm or raging sea. On a positive note, just outside our door there was an exit to the deck where we could set up the two folding chairs that we had brought. We enjoyed an evening cocktail there while watching the sunset on clear evenings. After classes the students used the decks and stairs as their jogging course, and they greeted us on their rounds.

Excitement was high the morning we left Nassau. Many parents had flown there to say a nervous goodbye to their children. Most of the students had never been abroad before, nor had they been away from their families for so long. Their parents ran along the quay as the ship slid out to sea. Six hundred students, thirty faculty, and twenty senior citizens stood waving on the decks as we headed toward the Florida Straits and South America.

Our ports included La Guaira, near Caracas, Venezuela; Salvador de Bahia, Brazil; Cape Town, South Africa; Mombasa, Kenya; Chennai (formerly Madras), India; Penang, Malaysia; Ho Chi Minh City (formerly Saigon), Viet Nam; Hong Kong, and Osaka, Japan. Ironically, the only time Granddaddy and I were a little seasick was when we crossed the Florida Straits. The hard cubes of ginger upon which we sucked got us through the passage while others were running for the bathrooms in their cabins.

Rather than provide an exhaustive summary of what happened in each port, I'll list the highlights: In Caracas, Venezuela, my students and I visited a school in one of the *rancho* communities in Caracas. We in the United States might refer to such a place as a "slum," but that word doesn't convey the understanding that the people who live in these places are frequently active in democratically run organizations that help them meet their basic needs for safety, food, health, and education. In Peru, as I explained earlier, the poorest areas were referred to as *pueblos jóvenes, or* young towns. In Brazil, the same kind of community, some of them perilously situated up mountain sides overlooking the gorgeous beaches, are called *favelas*. The children we saw in the Venezuelan school were bright, well-behaved, eager to learn, and excited to talk to our students. While in Venezuela, I also accompanied Granddaddy, who led a field trip to the cloud forest high above Caracas. The forest was not unlike the one you saw while we were in Costa

Rica. The birds were magnificent, with colors so brilliant I thought that God must have let loose all of His artistic powers when He created them.

Salvador, Brazil: Our visit to Salvador was my second. The first time was with Papi, when we flew there for a short visit from Recife, where your dad was born. In Salvador I accompanied my students to a *favela*. We learned about the social programs the residents had organized to improve their lives. In the evening we were treated to a *capoeira* demonstration where young men, dressed in white, loose-fitting pants, executed martial art moves that blended dance, acrobatics, and music. Our arrival coincided with Carnival, when scantily costumed Brazilians celebrate life in a prolonged extravaganza of music and dance.

Brazil is famous for its samba schools, most of which are in the *favelas*. Residents rehearse all year long, learning their music, dance routines, and preparing their costumes so they will be ready to parade for hours down streets that have been closed to cars. Our students were not prepared for the sights and sounds, especially the sight of nearly naked women and men the night before Lent began. (Lent is the forty-day period that used to be strictly observed in Catholic countries by small acts of self-denial in observance of Jesus' crucifixion and subsequent Resurrection, the feast we celebrate as Easter.) After the festivities in the upper city, we descended an elevator to the lower city. Unfortunately, as the door opened, we saw a small child who had passed out as a result of sniffing glue, a cheap way of getting high. (Salvador was one of the host cities of the 2014 World Cup. Understandably, many Brazilians resented the fortune that was allocated for the event while its government seemed to ignore the needs of the poor).

Cape Town, South Africa: We taught every day we were at sea, including weekends, so one of our longest stretches was the crossing of the South Atlantic. It was strange to stand before a class, trying to keep my balance, as the ship rocked back and forth. Stranger still was looking out the large windows in our classrooms and see the waves crashing against them. Sometimes we'd see flying fish.

Granddaddy had port duty on the ship the second night we were in Cape Town. He had the honor of greeting the famous Anglican bishop, Desmond Tutu, when he came aboard. Bishop Tutu addressed the entire shipboard community of nearly eight hundred persons, including crew. He spoke to us about the tragic history of Apartheid in South Africa, the economic, political, and social system that kept the races separated, reserving the lowest place in society for the black race. It was an oppressive system that destined blacks to bleak, unhealthy neighborhoods. Bishop Tutu was a trusted friend of President Nelson Mandela who, after having been imprisoned for twenty-seven years, led his people in a successful movement to eradicate Apartheid. The students' eyes were opened to the ways in which human beings can delude themselves by believing they are doing God's will while committing grave evil, instead.

In Cape Town, my students and I met with the women of the African National Congress who were preparing themselves to vote in upcoming elections. These were women who had frequently been imprisoned in their efforts to bring civil and human rights to their communities. We also visited a squatter camp of people who lived in crowded, unsanitary conditions, with as many as fifteen families sharing a communal latrine. Nevertheless, the children were eager to engage us, and the male students played soccer with them, using a ball made of plastic bags.

Toward the end of our stay in Cape Town, we traveled by bus to the Cape Of Good Hope, where the Indian and Atlantic oceans meet. We bought sandwiches for lunch at an outdoor cafe. All of a sudden, a baboon that had been sitting on the roof of the restaurant jumped down on a table and snatched a sandwich right out of a woman's hands. She was stunned. On the way home, we stopped at a little beach and enjoyed watching numerous Jack Ass penguins, a smaller version of the large Antarctic birds.

GRANDMOTHER, AT THE CAPE OF GOOD HOPE, SOUTH AFRICA, 1998

My students, especially the women, were very disturbed by the poverty they continued to see. As we arrived in Chennai, India, for example, women in brilliant cotton saris were bent over at the waist, sweeping the dock with short brooms made from palm fronds. Other women carried broken pieces of concrete on their heads from construction sites. Still others cleaned the troughs used for toilets near the dock. These women belonged to the Dalit class, formerly known as "untouchables." Despite living in a democracy, and despite the fact that the Indian Constitution forbids discrimination based on caste, prejudice is widespread. It's nearly impossible for poor Indians to rise above the class into which they were born because of the deep cultural traditions that separate human beings based on the station in life into which they were born. Castes are determined by one's work. If work is "ritually impure," that work is thought to pollute the soul, and pollution is contagious, thus the segregation.

BOYS IN A HOUSING DEVELOPMENT, CHENNAI, INDIA, 1998 (THEY'RE LOOKING AT YOU.)

As Granddaddy Joe and I headed south by train with several students, The Indian countryside was a pastel palette of greens and yellows. The fertile land produced rice and every kind of tropical fruit. We visited a wealthy family who had their own ornate Hindu temple. They served us delicacies we had never before tasted. Peacocks strutted through their compound. The owners were gracious, and I'd like to think they were generous to their many servants. Like many wealthy in our country, they probably never considered the fortunate circumstances into which they were born, including the wealth and education of their parents and the lighter color of their skin in a country where huge billboards advertise creams that will lighten it.

In Japan, Granddaddy Joe and I took a side trip to Kyoto, a lovely city known for its peaceful Buddhist temples and surrounding gardens. Later, I escorted a group of students to Hiroshima, where, along with Nagasaki, American pilots released atom bombs in August, 1945. To date it is the only time a nuclear weapon has been used in wartime. The American bombing brought an end to World War II that started after the Japanese bombed Pearl Harbor in Hawaii in December, 1941, when I was two-years-old.

While in Hiroshima, we visited the war memorial museum after which we felt emotionally overwhelmed. We emerged, however, into a park where it seemed every family in Hiroshima was celebrating Children's Day, a national holiday. Children were flying kites; others were making origami peace cranes. Families were dancing to folk music from other countries. I was pulled into a Bavarian folk dance by a happy group of costumed Japanese. The people who lived in Hiroshima, a city rebuilt from ashes, were joyfully celebrating life, knowing how fragile and precious it is.

Hiroshima Peace Park.

Photograph © Paul Quayle

POSTCARD FROM HIROSHIMA WAR MEMORIAL MUSEUM

Students studied for their final exams as we crossed the North Pacific on our way back to the United States. They were so excited about getting home they could barely concentrate. The morning of our arrival in Seattle, it seemed that every passenger stood on deck, waiting to get the first glimpse of America. It had been a long voyage. Long before this point, Granddaddy had started crossing the days off the calendar he had posted on the back of our cabin door.

## Cuba #3: Medical Assistance to "The Enemy"

**FRIENDS FROM MOBILE WHO BELONGED TO THE CUBAN HEALTH NETWORK INVITED US TO VISIT CUBA WITH THEM IN 2000 UNDER THE AUSPICES OF WORLD VISION, A HUMANITARIAN ORGANIZATION THAT HAD BEEN GRANTED U.S.** permission to visit the island. It would be my third visit and Granddaddy's first.

Included on our itinerary was a visit to a medical school in Havana. We were surprised to meet two dozen students from the United States who were studying to become doctors. The Cuban government provided them with free medical training, provided that they agree to return to the United States and practice in the poor communities from which they had come, the inner city of New York, for example. We also met with individual doctors who told us of the dire need for medicines in their country. Yes, everyone has access to community clinics, but the average Cuban lacks the specialized medical care we take for granted. The 1960 embargo, imposed one year after Fidel Castro and his followers won the revolution against the dictator Batista, continues to hurt the Cuban people and remains an obstacle to the very democratization the United States hopes to achieve.

## *September 11, 2001: Dissent May Also be Patriotic*

ON SEPTEMBER 11, 2001, TERRORISTS DESTROYED THE WORLD TRADE CENTER IN NEW YORK CITY, KILLING CLOSE TO 3000 PEOPLE, AND ALL THE WORLD TREMBLED, JUST WHAT THE TERRORISTS HAD HOPED TO ACCOMPLISH. Our nation, in an effort to capture or eliminate those responsible, who were thought to be hiding in the hinterlands of Afghanistan, went to war. Before achieving that end in Afghanistan, however, President George W. Bush took our nation to war in Iraq. Unfortunately for our country and the Middle East, Mr. Bush paid more attention to some old political friends who believed the United States had to control the oil in the Middle East. To do that, however, Saddam Hussein, the Iraqi president, would have to be eliminated. Bush advisors concocted links between Hussein and the World Trade Center terrorists. There were many in our nation who opposed an invasion of Iraq, fearing it would have tragic repercussions. We saw through the false arguments that Saddam had "weapons of mass destruction."

In September, 2002, when the rhetoric was heating up about a possible invasion of Iraq, I joined with other like-minded people in forming Pensacola Patriots for Peace. To protest against an invasion, we decided to hold a silent vigil every Friday from 12:00-1:00 p.m. at the Martin Luther King Plaza in downtown Pensacola. In March, 2003, however, the United States invaded Iraq, and we are still seeing the fall-out, including the emergence of ISIS (The Islamic State in Iraq and Syria), referred to now by its members as "The Islamic State," one of the deadliest threats to the Middle East and western nations, especially ours.

During the protests, many of us carried signs reading, "War is Not the Answer." In the early months, the drivers of passing cars frequently gave us the middle finger. Others shouted, "Get a job," despite the fact that several of our members worked and spent their lunch hour with us. Many of us had already retired. One day a driver of a big truck, with a rifle in the gun rack of his cab, made several sweeps around the Plaza. I held a clipboard in front of me to identify myself as the coordinator, just in case. As our years of protest wore on, the responses from drivers gradually changed. Many were now giving us the thumbs-up sign and honked in solidarity. Our demonstrations had become a barometer that reflected the changing mood of the country in regard to the endless strife in Afghanistan and Iraq. We continued our vigils for six years, till after the November, 2008 nomination of Barack Obama.

Since the invasion, the religious rivalries between Sunni and Shiite Moslems, that had been kept in check by Saddam Hussein, have manifested themselves in incalculable violence. Saddam was a very bad guy, but he didn't have "weapons of mass destruction," the pretext President George W. Bush used for going to war. We destroyed Iraq's infrastructure and dissembled its government and institutions. In the mayhem, much of the cultural artifacts of Iraq, once called Mesopotamia, the birth place of Abraham, the father of Judaism, Christianity, and Islam, have been destroyed.

I'd like to think that our protests, along with others in the United States and elsewhere, had something to do with the decision to end the war in Iraq. In retrospect, President Bush's proclamation, "Mission Accomplished," can only be seen as pitiful. He went to war a prideful, misinformed man who made the entire world less safe. He and his advisors probably still think they did the right thing. We saw it as our duty to dissent, but to dissent peacefully.

PENSACOLA PATRIOTS FOR PEACE. MARCH, 2003

## *In Retrospect: Family, Values, Hard Work, and Faith*

**I'VE HAD A RICH PROFESSIONAL LIFE THAT STARTED WITH A FIRM FAMILY FOUNDATION, FAITH, AND AN EXCELLENT EDUCATION.** I wouldn't be honest, however, if I didn't admit to some disappointment. After my two years in the Peace Corps, I harbored the desire to work in the diplomatic corps or with an international humanitarian organization. Not long after your dad and I returned to Milwaukee from Brazil, I applied to the Foreign Service but received a letter telling me that, at age thirty-four, I was "too old" to join the Service. I later learned that the letter referred to the "Junior" Foreign Service that only accepted candidates up to the age of thirty-one. But one moves ahead, despite the opportunities that might have eluded us. If we're alert, other windows open

So it was that, over twenty years later, fortified by my years of experience in Latin America and various publications, including my book on Nicaragua, I applied for the position of Director of International Education and Programs at the University of West Florida and got the job. Finally, my special interests and professional life merged. I wanted to be of service to others, and I think I fulfilled that goal. My degree programs were all top-notch, all demanding, especially while raising a young child. Despite the obstacles, I never stopped pursuing my international interests. If there were one recommendation I would make to you, it would be that you strive to know yourself, your values, and read widely.

Sophie, you're already an avid reader, especially of science fiction for young adults. I would encourage you to continue to expand your reading horizons and become familiar with literature that exposes you to different ways of thinking, to cultures different from your own, and to lives lived differently from your own. You and your brother already have the advantage of having traveled widely for your young ages, but reading widely also helps us test our own values against those of others. It helps us to understand that others have had problems similar to our own and have solved them. (I just learned that, while still a freshman in high school, you earned four out of five points in your Human Geography advanced placement test. I was thrilled that you were able to demonstrate your knowledge of other peoples and their countries at such a young age.)

Vincent, I'm delighted that you do lots of reading that enhances your knowledge of tropical fish, your primary interest at this writing. You're using reading as a tool to acquire knowledge in a specific area. I know that you love listening to the stories your parents have told you at bedtime, and that I've had the pleasure of telling you. These stories connect you to your family history, bringing to light the funny, sad, and significant events in our lives. There's much more of that pleasure inside the covers of books, especially good novels that describe adventures and human relations inside families other than our own. We're able to identify with the lives of others, see how they had to conquer their fears, and face up to difficult circumstances. Don't give those few ineffective teachers control over your reading habits. You're too good a reader for that, given that you knocked the top off the FCAT test.

As you both progress through high school, you may be attracted to extra-curricular activities or organizations that reflect your values. If so, don't hesitate to see what they're about. I understand you will have a community service requirement before you graduate from high school. Perhaps you can choose to volunteer with an organization that will employ your special gifts and talents. Last summer, for example, you visited a "no kill" animal shelter in Newland, North Carolina. You met Arlene and Dan, my friends who volunteer there three times a week. You seemed to enjoy playing with the kittens that were up for adoption, and I know how much you love dogs.

## *Making Difficult Decisions*

**I JUST FINISHED A BOOK WITH A SAD TITLE, BUT THE STORY IS UPLIFTING.** *The End of Your Life Book Club*, is the account of the hours Will Schwabe spent with his mother after she was diagnosed with pancreatic cancer at the same age I am now. They would go to the hospital together where she received chemotherapy. While waiting, they would recommend books to each other and discuss them, often drawing parallels between the books and their own lives. They had formed a book club of two. The author's mother had been employed by international relief agencies and had traveled the world, most recently to Afghanistan and Pakistan. She was especially involved with agencies that helped to improve the plight of refugees all over the world. Before she died she succeeded in establishing a program that would bring library books to children in rural Afghan villages.

In the memoir, the author, a book editor and journalist, wrote that, whenever he or his siblings had to make a difficult decision, their mother would advise them to take the path that was "reversible." She didn't mean that they should be timid about making rough choices, but that they should make decisions that, if necessary, could be modified, like finding the next exit on a freeway if you missed the right one. If we are afraid to take risks because we don't know the outcome, our decisions aren't reversible, because we're at a standstill, stuck in one place. If, on the other hand, we decide that the risk is worthwhile, and that there's a door through which we can exit in order to move forward, even in a different direction, we're still winners.

## *Treating Ourselves and Others: You Know the Rule*

**ABOVE ALL, SOPHIE AND VINCENT, TRUST YOURSELVES, YOUR GOODNESS, AND YOUR PLACE IN THIS WORLD.** Know that God loves you, and that you are deeply loved by your family. That in itself is a solid foundation for life. It's much easier to get in a slump and feel unloved and unappreciated than it is to talk hard to yourself about your abilities, intelligence, and, especially, the good fortune of having a family who loves and supports you, even though that support may not always show itself in the way you'd prefer.

I frequently got defensive when my mother criticized me for the way I dressed or wore my hair. I had no sense of humor about it, but I wish I had. I wish I had known how to deflect her criticism and get on with my life, but I would either snarl back or go to my room. Since then, I've learned how to say, for example, "I'm sorry you feel that way, but I am hurt when you speak to me that way." Such tactics are like tricks in a bag that help you to stand up for yourself while pushing back in a way you won't later regret. These tricks, however, are hard to remember when you're angry. During those times, walk away, calm yourself, and later return with an appropriate response. Such habits are also useful with friends and even teachers. I still have to remind myself that I shouldn't say things today that I can't take back tomorrow.

Sophie, this part is for you, and it has to do with our role as women. You've been born into a world where, at least in this country, women are supposed to be treated equally to men. There is still, however, a lot of subtle and not-so-subtle discrimination, and I have known a lot of it throughout my life, even since my retirement. And sometimes women treat *themselves* as if they're not equal in worth to men. We must learn to give ourselves the same respect, honor, and consideration we give men. Although this goal seems logical, it's difficult for many women to achieve because we generally want to avoid conflict, and it's easier to keep our hurt and resentment to ourselves than to speak out. Tennis has offered you the opportunity to cultivate a sense of your worth, mental agility, physical strength, and emotional stamina. Yes, you'll know what it is to lose a match now and then, but you'll also know the exhilaration of winning and have the satisfaction of knowing that you dedicated yourself to a sport despite the hardships of frequent practices in hot weather. You didn't know whether or not you'd make your high school tennis team but you showed up, over and over, despite big adjustments in your personal life, and those efforts paid off. A lot of young people lose opportunities to succeed in life simply by not showing up.

And Vincent, growing into manhood has its own challenges. Unfortunately, every society has stereotypes regarding the ideal man and woman. Every day we're bombarded with images of great looking, muscular jocks with gorgeous women looking up admiringly at them. If we're not careful, it's easy to think we *must* live up to those images, rather than concentrating on becoming the unique persons God made us to be. To further complicate things, many parents unintentionally discourage their boys from crying, expressing fear, or being honest about their emotions. As a result, young men often conceal what is in their hearts and learn to bury their deepest feelings. Some fathers or other male role models, such as those on TV or the movie screen, convey the stereotype that men have to be aggressive and tough. They haven't learned that, instead, women appreciate men who are intelligent, honest, confident, capable of showing tenderness, and, when needed, know how to use their physical strength with caution. You and your sister must remember you were made in the image of God. What an uplifting thought.

Since I began writing this memoir, Vincent, I've learned of your aquarium-related business. On your own, you have become an entrepreneur, someone who has a business vision and acts upon it. You did your research, inventoried your resources, analyzed the market, and set your prices based on your costs and a fair amount for profit. And you're only thirteen! Meanwhile, you're teaching yourself the science of tropical fish and the environment they require to thrive. You've had to take risks, experience disappointments, learned to negotiate with customers, all the while maintaining excellent grades, and playing soccer. What a guy!

## *Two Households Can't be Easy, but You're Champions*

**DESPITE DIFFICULTIES, YOU BOTH HAVE BEAUTIFULLY NEGOTIATED THE MAZE OF LIVING AS CHILDREN OF DIVORCED PARENTS.** Now you have a loving step-mom who helps with the transition from one household to the other. Maybe you will also have a step-dad. At this writing, Sophie will soon be a sophomore, and Vincent enters eighth grade. You will still contend with two households; two different ways of doing things; two wardrobes, and differing advice. Your parents are active people, with full professional lives. You are both, nonetheless, always foremost in their thoughts. If you ever feel that you can't cope, I hope you'll feel safe going to them. If there's a problem you can't solve alone, they will help you. And never forget that, as long as I live, I promise to be there for you, for whatever reason, and I promise not to judge you. Sometime it's easier to talk to someone who's not directly in the middle of the issue.

Midst the demands of your lives, both of you must have felt the need for quiet and calm. Respect this need and try to carve it out of your hectic lives. Even sitting outside for a few minutes, enjoying the nature in your backyard, while breathing deeply, can bring some peace of mind. And quiet prayer and meditation can help you face the demands of the day so you won't feel fragmented. Such time alone helps me to be more patient and loving to those around me. Taking time out to restore a peaceful spirit is a healthy habit for mind and body, one that I wished I had cultivated when I was your age.

## *Faith: The Foundation of My Life*

**THIS WILL SEEM STRANGE TO YOU BUT WHILE MY BROTHER AND I WERE AT ST. ANNE'S GRADE SCHOOL, WE ATTENDED DAILY MASS, AND ON SUNDAYS, WE ATTENDED MASS WITH OUR PARENTS.** We also went to confession every two weeks. I was always relieved after confessing my sins and receiving absolution. It felt like I was starting a new life, that my future was bright, and that I'd never, for example, be disrespectful to my mother again. But, of course, I would, and that misdeed and other new ones would remain on my conscience until my next confession. It was not that I felt I could do anything I wanted because confession would take care of it. Instead, I trusted that God would forgive me if I asked for his help to become a better person.

I don't go to confession much anymore, but when I think I've done something to offend another, I apologize to them, and every night I pray, sometimes on my knees, for you and all your family, asking that God keep you safe and well. There are many other family and friends for whom I pray, including Granddaddy who has suffered from chronic pain for so many years. Now I'm also praying for his daughter Rebecca, who has cancer. Of late I've been praying for President Obama because he faces so many urgent issues, especially in the Middle East. I also pray for myself, so that each day I become a more loving and compassionate person.

Prayer is a great consolation in my life. I don't pretend that my prayers are always answered. Instead, I think my prayers make me more aware of how I must change. After prayer, although frequently not right away, I feel inspired to take action in one way or another. I usually feel a lightening of my spirit, and my hope is increased. It's a relief to share my burdens with God and not keep all my worries to myself.

I don't think I ever questioned my faith as a young child, nor why I had to go to church so often. It simply was what my family and all those I knew did. Like you and your family, we prayed before meals, although we always said the same prayer, preceded and followed by the Sign-of-the-Cross:

Bless us, oh Lord, and these thy gifts, which we are about to receive, from thy bounty, through Christ, our Lord, Amen. (All those commas slowed us down so we could think about what we were saying.)

During the month of May, we prayed the rosary as a family in front of the May altar in our apartment over the bakery. We placed a statue of Mary in a mirrored alcove in our China cabinet. Mom said we could pick the flowers that hung outside of people's fences. On the way home from school, we'd cut through the alleys that ran along the fences of people's back yards and hope that we'd see some flowers sticking out. We must have known the owners wouldn't be happy to see us pick their flowers because we'd pick them and run like crazy. I continued to pray the rosary before falling asleep each night in Peru. (More often than not, I'd fall asleep before finishing.) Even now there's a rosary tucked away in my purse.

I believe that faith is a wondrous gift that helps us to know what is really important in life, helps us to be decent human beings who care about one another, helps us through difficult times, and gives us hope in the future. I'd never say that someone can't acquire these qualities without faith in God, but it has brought me through many dark, tough times. My prayer is that you and your brother will maintain your connection to the religion into which you were baptized at St. Joseph Catholic Church in Pensacola, and that, at some time in the near future, you will explore its long history so that you will understand and appreciate what may seem incomprehensible now.

After all the theology I've studied and read in my life, and after seventy-five years of life, I can boil down the essence of my faith to a sentence or two: I believe that Jesus Christ showed us how to live, love, forgive, and pointed out to us what is important and what is frivolous in life. He also taught us how to pray. I believe that, if we want to understand who or what God is, all we need to do is study the way Jesus lived and allow His life be a model for our own. Scripture, especially the New Testament, helps us learn about His life. In the Mass, we not only hear His words, we participate in the mystery of the last supper when we receive Communion. Mass helps me get centered in the midst of the worldly demands of each day. At Mass I consider my life in terms of the lessons Jesus provided through His words and His life.

I think that your parents, all three of them, are largely the people they are, in terms of their goodness and compassion, because of their past religious upbringing. Yes, they have drifted away from traditional practices, but I believe that their religious backgrounds had a strong role in developing their moral codes. This is never to say that, had they been raised Protestant, Jewish, Muslim, or atheist, that they would not have possessed the same qualities, but that in their respective lives, the religion with which they were raised has been a quiet influence. I say this knowing full well the crimes of a minority of priests who have betrayed their faith, and those bishops who protected them. They betrayed God and the people they were meant to serve. They represented the Church, but they were *not* the Church. I have known many dedicated, compassionate, and courageous priests, many of whom worked among the poorest peoples of the world. It is a shame that they have suffered because of others' crimes.

I pray that you and your brother will have the source of strength that faith in God imparts. I want you to look at the night sky and be awed that our ever-expanding universe, too complex to be grasped by even the best scientists, covers you, that you are an integral part of that universe, and, like the universe, you are a miracle of creation, not an accident. For both Granddaddy and me, the miracle of evolution is a manifestation of the existence of God. I am grateful that my church recognizes that evolution is completely compatible with belief in God.

I hope you will understand, at a gut level, that the cats and dogs you love, the dolphins you swam with, Sophie, the lizards, snakes, and tropical fish you tend, Vincent, are all part of God's creation. I want you to be amazed when you see a bumble bee insert its entire body into the brilliant yellow or orange center of the Jewelweed to sip its nectar while pollinating it so it will propagate. I want you to feel God when you're at the top of Grandfather Mountain, looking out at the lush forests below. I want you to see the face of God in a tiny, new-born baby.

Henry David Thoreau, an abolitionist and naturalist whom you may already have studied, wrote a book called "Faith in a Seed." Like the seed that has within it all the DNA of the adult plant it will become, you have a spirit receptive to faith. Like that seed, your faith needs the soil, sun, and the rain of quiet moments to grow. Prayer has many forms. Sometimes it's simply feeling God in the beauty of creation, or it can take the form of petition when we ask for guidance or special help with a problem, or pray for a loved one. Sometimes we utter a prayer of gratitude for all the good fortune in our lives, for our families, food, shelter, and education, knowing that most people throughout the world have so much less.

## *In Closing: A Grandmother's Blessing*

**DEAREST GRANDCHILDREN, THERE'S MUCH MORE IN MY HEART THAT I WOULD HAVE LIKED TO SHARE WITH YOU.** I wanted so much to make these notes sound informal as though I were again telling you stories at bedtime, but I fear that, in certain places, I got carried away. Sophie, during your 2013 summer visit with us in North Carolina, I still wanted to tuck you in, sing a song, tell you stories, but I felt, perhaps mistakenly, that I had to respect your age and preferences. As the fourteen-year-old girl you were then, it's natural that you would have been setting new boundaries for yourself. One could even call them "barriers" as you stake out your territory, discover yourself, and achieve autonomy. Sensing this need in you, I kissed you goodnight; you watched a little more TV, and I went to bed without telling you the stories or praying with you as I had just done with your younger brother. I was insecure about this arrangement and came close to asking you if you still might like a story, or if I might pray with you, but I thought better of it.

You are both on the brink of discovering an exciting—and sometimes dangerous—world. You will have to determine your own paths, navigate the choices, take risks, and an occasional plunge, while my years are numbered. With this memoir, I hope to give you something of myself, perhaps some nuggets of wisdom resulting from a life that's been full of joy and a good dose of sorrow.

I'm confident that you will know much happiness in your lives. You'll learn, however, that what makes us appreciate the happy moments are those sad times we've also known. You'll also realize that the pleasure we experience from having money and the right kind of house, car, clothes, and electronics is fleeting, fragile, and vulnerable to events outside of ourselves. Happiness that is more permanent comes from the knowledge that we are using our gifts in the service of others. We also know happiness when we are fully using our gifts and talents, when we've discovered what we love to do and do it.

Time disappears when the tasks we undertake provide satisfaction and pleasure. We forget our problems, and we are at peace. Sophie, you've known that contentment when you used your artistic talent to painstakingly carve walking sticks here in the mountains. You might have considered such an undertaking insignificant, but you left for us and others useful objects of great beauty. And this summer of 2014 you gave us a drawing of a delicately shaded rose-colored flower against what seemed an exquisite, Oriental background. Vincent, you know the same pleasure when you've been fishing and have brought fish home to feed your family. Watching you fish, I've always been moved by your persistence and by your concentration on the movement of the water and line. It seems that you are absorbed in each moment, never aware of the clock.

Coincidentally, I recently came across an old anthology in our North Carolina bookcase. I was in sixth grade when its editor, Lillian Eichler Watson, published it in 1951. In it I found a quote on happiness by J.B. Priestley.

> To me there is in happiness an element of self-forgetfulness. You lose yourself in something outside yourself when you are happy; just as when you are desperately miserable you are intensely conscious of yourself....

Sophie, I have loved you from the time of your birth, and that love has steadily grown over the years as I see you flower into beautiful womanhood. In a few years you'll be choosing a university and launching an exciting new life, perhaps in Science and Math or in the Arts, since you're talented in both areas. Vincent, I bonded with you from the first moment I held you in my arms as a baby. You wouldn't stop crying, and I was desperate to make you feel secure and loved. You are a delightful young man, bright, adventurous, loving, and curious. I am filled with hope when I consider the rewarding futures that await you and your sister.

You both have a rich and diverse ancestral past. All the family members who came before you are part of that past, but you and God will compose your futures. My hope is that the Creator will grant me many more healthy years so that I may witness the miraculous unfolding of your lives.

I want to thank you for reading this memoir, even though you may have only read parts of it. Perhaps the title, *Water Skiing on the Amazon*, is a metaphor for my life. I think of one who water skis as adventurous, one who rides over both smooth and turbulent waters, maybe apprehensive about the deep waters beneath and of what might lurk there, but still ready to "test" them.

Your loving grandmother,
Montezuuma, North Carolina
September, 2014

AT HOME IN PENSACOLA, CHRISTMAS, 2000

Made in the USA
Columbia, SC
29 July 2024